# Uncovering You 5: Confessions

## (Uncovering You, #5)

D1489094

Scarlett Edwards

This book is a work of fiction. All names, characters, locations, and incidents are products of the author's imagination, or have been use fictitiously. Any resemblance to actual persons living or dead, locales, or events is entirely coincidental.

UNCOVERING YOU #5: CONFESSIONS

Edited by Gail Lennon.
Cover design by Scarlett Edwards.
Interior design by Scarlett Edwards.

Published by Edwards Publishing, Ltd.

Edwards Publishing

477 Peace Portal Drive

Suite 107-154

Blaine, WA 98230

ISBN: 978-0-9937370-8-4

.

# *Uncovering You 5: Confessions*

by Scarlett Edwards

Edwards Publishing

# Chapter One

Cold. Always, so cold.

I huddle into myself and try to stop my teeth from chattering.

It's no use. What little heat my body produces is powerless against the AC blasting into the room.

I can't see anything. All my familiar comforts are gone. All I know is the shape of the armchair.

I don't even have a blanket. Or a cloth I can use as one.

I thought my captivity by the pillar was bad. Hah! This is worse. I'm trapped on this tiny island. I can't move. I can't walk around. I can't do anything. I am barely alive.

All at once, the lights above me sputter on. I wince

and shy back, covering my eyes with my forearm. My heartbeat doubles in raw anticipation.

Once a day, the lights come on. They stay on for exactly fifteen minutes, Jeremy told me. That's all the time I have to run to the bathroom, empty my chamber pot, quickly shower, and change into something fresh for his arrival.

There's no fighting it. I can't refuse. I push myself up, my whole body trembling, and grab the disgusting, lidded, clay container. I hear the contents slop around inside as I hurry toward the bathroom.

I dump the chamber pot into the toilet. The first time I did it, the smell was enough to make me vomit. I almost—almost—made the mistake of trying to clean up, before remembering that time is short. Once the clock is up, my collar is reactivated. This means that, if I'm not in my chair in time…

I shudder. I didn't have time to shower that day. When Jeremy came for his nightly visit and found me reeking of vomit, he was not happy.

What happened next is a memory that I never want to revisit.

I turn on the shower, hot. Hot as it can go. I step in, forcing myself to stand under the scalding stream.

The shower used to be my sanctuary. The hot water, a method of control. I could stand there and feel the water burn my skin. I could control the pain I felt and — consciously — opt for more.

Stonehart caught on to what I was doing after just three days. He had forbidden me from self-harm before. He did not like me breaking his rule.

The shower does not work as it used to. He had someone come in and fix it so that the hottest stream of water was not enough to burn me. I hate him for it.

But, I have to admit, in a futile, hopeless way, that it was probably for the best. Jeremy was looking out for me. He did not want me hurt.

"Hah!" The laugh bursts out of me. The ludicrousness of that thought is appalling. None of this would be happening were it not for him. I wouldn't need to burn myself under scalding water were it not for him.

The heat seeps under my flesh and into my very bones. I count off the minutes in my head. There's no warning before the lights turn off and my collar is activated. No indication that time is running short.

The only thing I can rely on to get back before the time is my mind.

At thirteen minutes and ten seconds, I step out and quickly dry myself. I grab a new robe — the only thing I'm allowed to wear these days — and throw it over my shoulders. I pick up the chamber pot and turn for the door...

I stop. *Shit!* I forgot to brush my teeth.

*Thirteen minutes and fifty seconds.*

I don't have enough time. But if I get some mouthwash...

I rummage through the cupboard and pull a bottle out. I glug some down and swirl it around, then spit it into the sink.

*Fourteen minutes, ten seconds.*

I'm running out of time. My heart starts to race. I grab the chamber pot and rush out.

*Fourteen minutes thirty seconds. Fourteen minutes thirty-one seconds.*

The chair's up ahead. The lights are still on. Still,

this is going to be close.

*Forty seconds. Forty-one seconds. Forty-two seconds.*

I start to sprint. The clock in my mind is not infallible. Who knows if my timing's off? It could be late, and then—

My wet foot slips against the floor and slides out from under me. I cry out as I hurtle to the floor.

*Forty-three seconds. Forty-four seconds…*

No! No! I look up at the chair. It's so close…

*Forty-five seconds. Forty-six seconds…*

I push myself up, chamber pot forgotten, and hurl myself to the safety of the armchair.

I do not make it.

All the lights go off. And, at exactly the same moment, a wild torrent of electricity pulses into me.

I shriek in pain and crash to the floor. My limbs flail around me.

The last thought I have before I pass out is of that cruel, deceiving number:

*Forty-six seconds.*

***

I wake up slowly, drifting from the realm of sleep into the world of the living.

My body feels like it's made of rubber. All my muscles are loose, but somehow heavy at the same time. It's not a comfortable feeling.

There are hands on me. Touching me. Holding me. Lifting my body, directing me up. Moving me.

It takes my brain too long to realize what is

happening. When understanding finally clicks, my eyes burst open — to pitch blackness.

But those hands are still on me.

I try to fight them, desperate to break out of their grip. My muscles are slow to respond. It's as if my entire body is being pressed down by a thick layer of honey.

"Easy. Easy, Lilly," the voice soothes.

That voice. That horrible, smooth, terrible male voice.

*Stonehart is here.*

"Easy now. Relax. I'm taking care of you. You've had a little accident."

Revulsion and hatred and disgust course through me at his nonchalant choice of words.

"I'm just helping you back up," he says. I feel

myself settling into something soft. The chair? It must be.

"There you go."

I open my mouth to speak, but not a single word comes out. It feels like my tongue is made of wet cotton.

Stonehart brushes my jawline with strong, warm fingers as he regards me closely. I cannot see him, but I feel his proximity. "Let's try to avoid situations like that in the future, hmm?" he suggests. "You know you have to be back in time."

Then he stands up, pulls back, and walks away.

Only when his footsteps fade out of hearing do I collapse to my side and cry.

# Chapter Two

I wake up an indeterminate amount of time later.
My previous grogginess is gone. My body feels like
my own again.

I move my arms and legs without that strange
restriction. *What happened? Did he drug me again?*

I take a cautious sniff of air. There's no lingering
smell. It means Stonehart helped me out of that
soiled robe.

I bury my face in my hands and try not to sob.
This is humiliating. Who would do this to another
person? Who would make me live through this
nightmarish darkness twice?

The cold surrounds me again. I stuff my hands
into my armpits to try to keep my fingers warm. My

ears are freezing.

*How much longer?* I think in despair. *How much more of this will I have to take?*

***

"Open yourself to me."

His voice echoes in the dark. It's strong and virile.

I have to obey.

Shaking and trembling — not from fear, but from the incessant cold — I slide down in the chair and spread my legs. Already, my mind retreats to a faraway place.

He pushes into me. The hard rigidness of his cock makes me give a little gasp. I know better than to fight or resist in any way.

*Why would I?* Stonehart always gets what he wants. Challenging that only makes things worse.

So I lie there, wretched and forgotten, allowing him to pump his hips into my limp body. I am nothing but an empty vessel to him. A warm place to stick his dick.

Although even the *'warm'* part could be contested.

I close my eyes and wait for this nightmare to be over.

\*\*\*

The lights come on again. I sit up, slightly dizzy, a little nauseous. I notice the blood running down my leg.

*Oh, God.*

18

I look at the seat of the chair. It's stained red.

*Oh God, how didn't I notice before?*

But I know perfectly well how. After Stonehart left, I huddled up and let my mind go blank. Awake or asleep, it makes no difference. As long as I did not *think* things were... well, they were...

I mean, they were...

They just *were*. I can't say they were tolerable, or horrible, or anything at all. They just *were*.

I can't allow myself to attach emotions or feelings to them. Maybe once I get out of this, I'd be better suited to reflect. Right now, with no definitive end in sight, all I can do is *exist*.

Kind of like a slug.

After my shower, I find a box of tampons and bring them back with me. I also carry an extra towel to place over the stain. Jeremy — Stonehart — whatever, I don't even know why I don't think of him by his first name anymore — forbade me from using towels as blankets. He said that all things have their proper use, and I was not to bastardize that.

This, I hope, is different.

The lights turn off after I'm comfortably settled in my chair. I give myself only ten minutes now, to shower and come back.

I don't want to suffer any more "*accidents*."

# Chapter Three

How long has it been? A week? Two? Maybe more?

My bet is on *"more"*.

I can feel the remaining pieces of my sanity slowly crumbling away. What is an existence like this worth? Where do I find the strength or will to keep fighting?

I scoff. I'm not fighting. Fighting would be foolish. Idiotic.

Fighting would earn me further punishment.

Is this what will become of my life for the next five years? A state halfway between a zombie and a human?

Everything I ever held dear has been stripped

away. If Stonehart's goal is to show me how little control I have left, he doesn't need to do anything more.

In the back of my mind, I wonder what happened to Rose. It's the first time in this second — or is it third? — imprisonment that I allow myself to think about the kindly woman.

Does she know where I am?

*Undoubtedly.*

Has she done anything to help?

*Undoubtedly not.*

And I thought I could count on her as a friend. I thought —

*No.* I stop myself from sliding any further down that slippery slope. Rose has no influence over Stonehart. I remember the dove. Rose can't do anything to help me while I'm in here.

It's not her fault. I cannot hold it against her. If I ever see her again—

I stop myself once more. *Will* I ever see her again? I can't be sure. I can't be sure of anything while trapped in this dark hole.

Stonehart wants me to break. I laugh. I'm already broken. I am so far gone that no amount of reflection or soul-searching will ever rescue me from the pits of despair.

I have no friends, no love, no goals or hopes or dreams or aspirations.

Stonehart has squeezed all of those out of me.

It's just sleep, wake, *rape*.

\*\*\*

23

I come to face down on the chair, and realize that I'm being fucked.

It's a strange sensation to wake to, especially since I know that it's been going on for some time. I can hear Stonehart's pants behind me. He did not start recently.

He's been going at it for a while.

It's a testament to how far I've fallen that I don't even care. It's a testament to how numb I've become.

I don't let the mixed feelings of pain and pleasure distract me. I simply close my eyes and wonder if I can drift back into sleep...

***

My meals are brought to me on a cart. Stonehart wheels them in himself. He leaves them close by, within arm's reach, and then leaves.

Even though he does not speak when he does it, and I cannot see a thing, I know that it's him. I've become so accustomed to his presence that I could pick him out if I were blindfolded and in a crowd of fifty.

Part of it is the way he breathes. His breathing is slow and controlled. It reflects the purpose he seems to find in whatever he does.

His breathing also mirrors his voice. I wonder if he trained himself to speak the way he does. That baritone rumble seems to come effortlessly to him. However, for some reason, I can picture him practicing it as a youth.

***

I yearn for someone to speak to. I need a confidante. A friend. I feel so utterly alone and so completely useless.

What have I done to improve my position with Stonehart since I was first given access to his mansion? Nothing. Nothing at all. From the minute I entered his house, it's been nothing but blunder after blunder after blunder.

First there was the wine bottle that I threw at his face. The memory evokes a brief smile. That was fun.

Then there was the surveillance room disaster. The dove. The nighttime adventure in his office. *Falling asleep* on the day I knew to expect him.

I've long since come to grips with the fact that

anything bad that happens to me is my own fault. Would Stonehart have ever punished me if only I'd done what he asked?

No. If only I'd been a little smarter, a little more astute… things could be different now.

I yearn for the days when the TGBs meant something. Stonehart claims he is a man of his word, but he promised me that TGBs earned would not be taken away.

The irony hurts so much I want to cry. He *did not* take them away.

He just snatched away all the freedoms they granted.

*What a stupid system*, I think to myself. *Why would he even introduce them if he never meant to use them properly?*

*Probably as a way to taunt me. As a way to tempt me with the promise of ultimate freedom. As a way to ensure my behavior.*

I flip over on the chair and scoff. He didn't need to tempt me with TGBs to get me to behave. All he needed to do was leave me in the dark like this two or three more times.

Because right now, I am sure that I will never, ever do anything to displease Stonehart. Ever again.

He doesn't even know what this latest stint has done to me. My resolve to get back at him? Gone. My resolution to get revenge? Vanished. I know, in my heart of hearts, that the best I can hope for is to simply tread carefully enough in the next five years to avoid finding myself in the dark again.

Discomfort and discontent boil up inside of me. *Why was I so stupid before?* In the days before I was bound to this chair, I had it made. I was living in a magnificent mansion with a stunning view of the sea. I had access to every nook and cranny on the property—well, *almost*.

Why couldn't that have been enough?

*Because I'm a stubborn idiot, that's why.*

Was my life really so bad? I mean, sure, I had to make myself available for Stonehart whenever he wanted. But, that was a minor inconvenience— especially compared to what is happening now.

At best, it was absolutely wonderful. I remember the way he made me feel the one time we made love in his bed…

Of course, that was all a lie. It was just his way of exerting his dominance over me.

Now, he does not even treat me like a living

human.

Thinking back, I have no idea what right I had to complain. I mean, maybe I had no access to the outside world. But, was it really that bad? I know there are people — monks, hermits — who purposefully remove themselves from society. Couldn't I have just thought of my isolation the same way?

*No. Because it was not your* choice.

I shrug the uncomfortable thought away. No matter what, it was better than this.

I try to imagine what will happen when I'm finally let out. Stonehart said we would be "starting from the beginning." Does that mean all my TGBs are gone? Does that mean I'm to be confined by the pillar again?

Even that would be an improvement. I won't

complain. Maybe I'll even be allowed to see Rose again. I'm sure she'll be happy to chat. At least, I hope she will. I need to ask her about Charles, and the guesthouse I saw her leaving…

I yawn. Fatigue is washing over me. There's no point fighting it. I close my eyes and fall into a deep sleep.

***

I wake to overwhelming brightness. Alarms go off in my head as I jerk upright. I've slept through part of my fifteen minutes!

I curse and scramble up. How long do I have?

Then I notice something that astounds me: The light is coming from *outside*.

31

*Holy shit.*

I spin around.

The blinds are open. Cold winter sunshine floods the room.

I can't believe it. I stare out the window, and bring a trembling hand to my collar.

*Is that it? Is this… over?*

I hear footsteps behind me and whirl back. My senses are on high alert.

I see Stonehart approaching. I instinctively shy back into the depths of the armchair.

He smiles as he looks me over. It's a small smile, one that barely touches his lips. But it's reflected in his eyes, as well.

He looks strong and virile and powerful. His hair is a little shorter than I remember. Maybe he just had it cut. Or maybe not. I could never see his face in the dark.

He stops before me and glances around the room. Hatred and disgust fill me at the sight of him. But, beneath those emotions lies a twinge of fear.

His smile broadens as he sits next to me. I press my back as far into the chair as I can. I do *not* want him this close, not in broad daylight, not when I can see every handsome detail of his face.

He looks at me for a long, quiet moment. To my credit, I don't flinch. I catch a whiff of his cologne. It's light, almost like the memory of a scent. But it amplifies his personal aroma, somehow underscoring his masculinity.

To think, I used to respond to that smell.

Now, nothing could be farther from the truth.

"Lilly." Stonehart's voice is gentle. He lifts a hand to touch my cheek. My strength fails, and I shy away.

His face falls. His hand drops down. He looks genuinely hurt.

"You don't want me to touch you?" he asks.

I balk. How do I respond to that?

*No shit I don't want you to touch me*, I think, *but I can't very well come out and say that, can I?*

Instead, I give a resigned sigh, and lean slightly toward him, granting implicit permission.

He gives a sad smile. The tips of his fingers brush my jawline. It's a soft, gentle touch that makes goosebumps erupt along my skin.

"You know," he says, staring deep into my eyes, "Rose has been asking to see you. It would please me very much to grant her that request."

I don't answer. It's not like I'm locking myself in here. Everything happens at Stonehart's discretion.

The thought makes me sad.

"I told her that I would talk to you and ask what you think of that request," he continues. He tilts my chin up and makes me look at him. "So, Lilly? What do you want me to say?"

"I think —" I swallow. "I think I would like that."

I jerk my gaze away.

From the corner of my eye, I see Stonehart's face brighten. "Good," he says. "I was hoping you would respond positively." He takes a breath. "You know, Lilly, it gives me no great pleasure keeping you in here. I look at the state you're in —" His eyes run over me. " — and can't help but feel that part of this is my fault."

My hackles rise and my backbone snaps into place. *Part* of it is *his* fault?

*Try "all," you motherfucking bastard!* I think.

Wisely, I don't give voice to my thoughts.

Stonehart rocks his head from side to side, as if trying to see me from a better angle. "But then," he chuckles humorlessly, "I remember what you did to get yourself here, and that tendril of guilt flutters away."

I force myself to meet his eyes again. My strength is returning. I don't know if he's serious or not. It *sounds* like he's mocking me. But, his voice is chock-full of the deepest sincerity.

I remember the strength of his poker face, and decide, *he is making fun of me.* I tell myself not to take it to heart.

"Lilly," he says again, his hand dipping down to trace the collar around my neck, "You are so very beautiful. Why do you force me to do these things to you? If only you'd *behave* —" his fingers come to rest at the soft spot beneath my chin and he tilts my head up, " — we could have the pleasure of truly enjoying each other's company."

Enjoying each other's company? Is the man completely insane?

My backbone is set in place and anger starts to fume inside of me.

He tilts his head to the side and smiles. "Oh, I know that look," he says. He raises both his hands in mock-surrender. "I've said something to upset you. Please, don't throw another wine bottle at me."

Then he laughs, a great, rich laugh, as if he's just made the most magnificent joke in the world.

"But really," he says through one last chuckle. "Please don't force me to put you in this situation again, Lilly. I worry about you when you're in here. You don't know how much trouble I have sleeping when I know you're cold, alone, and lonely."

"Is that why you come in and rape me every night?" I spit in his face. Then I gasp, and throw both hands over my stupid mouth. My eyes widen in fear.

*Idiot!* A voice cries out in my head. *Fucking idiot! You're a glutton for punishment, aren't you?*

I wait for the oncoming explosion… and am caught by surprise when the only reaction that Stonehart gives is a widening of his smile. "I knew you had some spirit left," he says, sounding pleased — pleased! — by the revelation.

He stands. "The collar is deactivated once more, Lilly-flower. Your freedoms have been reinstated.

You are welcome to come and go as you please. And I, for my part, will do my best not to provoke reactions in you that will warrant future punishment." He pauses. "I like seeing you happy and free."

Then he turns back. "It's a quarter to two," he says. "Today is a rare day off work for me, but I won't be calling upon you until six. Rose, you, and I are going to enjoy a wonderful dinner prepared by Charles. Rose is dying to see you. The only request I make is that you dress appropriately for the occasion."

He stoops low and picks up my chamber pot. His nose wrinkles in disgust. "I'll get rid of this awful thing for you."

***

I wait until Stonehart is really gone before cautiously placing a foot on the cold, tile floor.

The AC is off. Thank God. Sunshine from outside is starting to warm up the room.

I push myself from the chair and stand. A brief wave of dizziness comes over me. *Not enough carbs,* I think.

I take a deep breath and wait for it to pass. This is it. I've survived the worst that Stonehart could throw at me.

*Twice.*

The thought grants me precious little satisfaction. I know the reason is that Stonehart was *right*.

He was right when he said I find myself in such situations only because of my own stupidity. How different would things have been if I hadn't fallen asleep when Stonehart came back from his trip? Where would I be, right now? What type of progress could I have made with him?

I wander to the huge window and look outside. It's a dull, grey day. A thick sheet of clouds blocks the sun. The ocean is deceptively peaceful.

It feels like I'm trapped in the eye of a storm.

Just as I'm turning back, I catch my reflection in the glass. I turn and face it.

"You're a survivor," I whisper. "You've gotten through everything Stonehart has thrown at you, barely the worse for wear."

That might not be entirely true. But, I need to make myself believe it. Otherwise, I'm afraid I'd risk a real mental breakdown.

When I start the shower, a few minutes later, my hand reaches automatically to turn the heat up as high as it can go.

I stop myself halfway through the motion.

*I am not a prisoner in the chair any longer*, I tell myself. I settle on making the water a pleasant, unhurried warmth.

I step out a long time later and leisurely towel myself dry. I walk to the powder room and open the towel to examine my body.

*Hmm*. I'm a bit skinnier than I remember. But I haven't lost my curves. That's a wonder. I haven't been eating a lot during my most recent stay in the dark.

I check my hair. It's gotten longer than I usually like to keep it.

With a start, I remember the cameras watching me from the other side of the mirror. I start to close the towel. But, then I stop, take a deep breath, and force myself to relax.

Like a starlet, I smile wide for the invisible audience, and turn away.

Freedom has rejuvenated me. Sure, I may not be free in the true sense of the word. I think I've given up on that possibility, anyway — at least in the short-term. For now, I'm happy enough not to be restricted to that damned chair.

I walk back to the sunroom, wrapped in a fluffy navy robe. It might be exactly the same as the one I wore most days during my confinement, but it *feels* different. Instead of the fabric being heavy and constricting, it's soft and consoling.

It's a wonder what a change of perspective can do

to your psyche.

I walk toward the bed. With a hysterical giggle, I launch myself onto the sheets. I roll around for a bit, then stretch wide and yawn deeply.

I've missed this bed. I never thought I would say that, not after those three days spent trapped on it — but three days are nothing compared to the length of time I was stuck in that chair.

I roll onto my front and prop my chin up. I stare at that chair.

*I hate you*, I think. *I hate you, you fucking goddamned chair.*

It's not just the reminder it gives that makes me loathe it. It's everything else it represents, too. That is the chair on which I fell asleep waiting for Stonehart . That is the chair I left the dove on before Stonehart found her. That is the chair that earned me that painful slap when Stonehart thought I'd asked Rose for it.

That chair has been nothing but bad news. I want it gone.

I stand up and push it toward the glass door. I turn the handle and prop the door open with my hip. I pause for a second, just to make sure there's no warning zap beneath my ear. When none comes, I haul the chair outside.

I stand back and admire my work. It's out of the sunroom.

But if I just leave it here, it'll never be out of my mind. I need to get it out my sight.

Tugging the sash of my robe to make sure it doesn't come undone, I set about pulling the heavy chair out of the way.

The feet make horrible scraping sounds against the cement, enough to wake the dead. I grit my teeth and endure it.

As I'm struggling with the chair, heaving and grunting while pulling it with no regard to where I'm going, I collide with somebody I did not even know was there.

I spin back, startled — and my heart sinks when I find Stonehart looking at me, his lips pursed in amusement.

"Jeremy," I say, flustered. I am suddenly aware of how ridiculous I must look. And of how easily finding me like this might set him off. "I didn't expect you."

"No," he says, his voice light and his eyes glittering with mirth, "clearly, you did not." He looks over my shoulder, at the chair. "What are you doing?"

I strain my ears to find a trace of malice in his voice, but there is none. I think I've become so accustomed to him being displeased with every little thing I do that it's a shock when he's not.

"Um," I blow out my cheeks and brush a stray strand of hair out of my eyes. I glance down at the stain on the seat and blanch despite myself. "I wanted to, er, clean it. Outside," I lie.

Stonehart laughs. "By yourself?" he asks. "You know, we have hired help for that."

"I didn't want to trouble Rose," I mumble.

"Not her." He clicks his tongue. "The woman would kill me if I suggested anything of the sort."

"She would… *what*?" I say, thrown off guard by the comment.

"It means, she wouldn't do it," he confides. "She would tell me off for even suggesting it. Have you seen her angry?" He mock-shudders. "I couldn't imagine a more formidable foe."

I stare at him. Here he is, talking to me as if the last few weeks hadn't happened. Talking to me like I am… a regular human being.

I will never be able to understand what makes the man tick.

"I noticed your struggle from upstairs." He motions to his bedroom windows overlooking the backyard. "I thought I would come down and offer my help."

"You? Help *me*?" I ask, somewhat aghast.

He laughs again. "It's an attempt at chivalry, Lilly."

I narrow my eyes in suspicion.

"So, what do you say?" he continues. "Would you like my help, or not? Although, looking at the state of the chair, I don't know how much success you'd meet cleaning it. May I suggest new upholstery, or perhaps a replacement chair?"

His eyes meet mine. Some of that intellect I was so impressed by when I first met him comes through. "I don't think you'll be eager to spend any more time on that one," he says softly.

I nod, a little dazed. "You're right. Thank you for the offer, Jeremy."

"Of course." He takes the chair by the back and lifts it as if it were weightless. Then, he glances at me, and I see an unexpected playfulness hidden in his eyes. "Your robe's come undone," he says. His eyes flicker down for a moment. "Your breasts are showing."

# Chapter Four

As I follow Stonehart with my arms firmly crossed over my chest, he updates me on the things I missed during my "*absence*". He terms it as lightly as if it were nothing more than a pleasant trip to the Bahamas.

His takeover of Dextran Technologies went through. He'd axed Esteban and appointed an interim CEO. The official word, he tells me, is that a search is being conducted for a permanent replacement. The way he looks at me when he says that, however, tells me that he does not intend to look far.

*He can't still mean to appoint me?* I wonder. *Why does he want me to think otherwise? The joke's gone on far too long.*

He leaves me alone to change. I spray a touch of perfume around my neck and behind my ears, and then put on a strapless red dress. It's the one I meant to meet Stonehart in.

When I come out of the sunroom a quarter to six, I find Rose waiting for me in the lobby. She races to me, and, all pretense forgotten, envelopes me in a monstrous hug.

"I've been so worried about you," she whispers in my ear as she holds me tight. Her eyes are moist with unshed tears. "I've been asking Mr. Stonehart about you day and night. He told me that you were unable to take visitors until further notice. I just *knew* something horrible had happened to you. And all of those damn cameras—"

She cuts off, and a look of shock flies over her face. Then she shakes her head and continues in a steely voice, "All of those *damned cameras* don't do me one iota of good because I don't have access to their recording. I had no idea what was happening to you. Oh! But look at you now, so pretty and beautiful. I knew nothing could break your spirit." She takes my hand and leads me to the dining room.

Stonehart is seated at the table, next to a man I've seen before but have not met. He is the one who drove Rose away from the guesthouse.

They both rise when they see me enter. Stonehart smiles and says, "Lilly, this is Charles. He apologizes for not meeting you earlier, but it always takes him time to warm up to strangers."

Charles bows his head.

"It's nice to meet you, Charles," I say, extending my hand.

Something very strange happens. Instead of

taking it, Charles looks at Stonehart, almost as if asking for permission. Stonehart gives a slight nod, and then makes a series of motions with his hands.

*Sign language*, I think, startled.

A smile erupts on Charles's face. He makes a few different gestures back, then reaches out and shakes my hand warmly, using both of his.

Then, before I can say another word, he bows his head again and ducks out of the room.

"Charles was always very shy," Rose says from behind me. I look back at her. "It took me a full two years before he would even glance my way, when we first came under Mr. Stonehart's employment."

Stonehart chuckles and pulls out my chair for me. "But he's the finest chef I've ever had the privilege of knowing," he says.

I sit on the chair in a kind of disbelieving daze. This all feels so very normal. Domestic, even. Nothing at all about Stonehart's behavior gives any hint of what he'd been subjecting me to for weeks.

Charles brings out the appetizers shortly. Then, he surprises me by sitting down himself, beside Rose. When she takes his hand, a smile blossoms on my lips.

*I was right.*

Stonehart clears his throat. We all look at him. "Shall I say grace, then?" he asks.

Rose smiles and holds out her hand. He takes it, and then links his other one with mine. I am too off balance to do anything except reach across the table to hold Charles' hand.

The whole thing is over before I can blink. After Stonehart gives his little speech, he leans to me and, shielding his mouth with one hand, whispers, "I'm not a religious man." He tilts his head toward Charles. "But he is, and this was the only way he'd agree to join us for dinner."

I give a slight nod, still uneasy. I feel tense and anxious about the whole affair. This isn't real. It can't be real. It's all an act.

But, how did Stonehart find such willing performers in Rose and Charles?

"You know, dear," Rose says as we start to eat, "I've been wanting to see you for so long. You really mustn't take yourself away from us like that again." She gives Stonehart a brief but pointed look. I'm certain she knows who's really at fault.

But, why the pretense? Why can't she come out and say what she really thinks?

*Why didn't she help me?*

The only reason I can think of is that Stonehart has something on her. He is a master manipulator. Her unwavering loyalty to him must rely on something I don't know about.

Stonehart smiles as he brings his wine to his lips. "You have a formidable ally in Rose," he tells me. "Did you know, she actually threatened to resign if she didn't see you for Christmas dinner tonight?"

I choke on the piece of food in my mouth. *It's Christmas?*

I feel everyone's eyes on me as I cough. I take a sip of water to regain my voice and look at Rose. "You really did that?"

She makes a shooing motion with one hand. A touch of color enters her cheeks. "It was nothing."

"Oh no," Stonehart says. "It was quite something. Rose stormed into my office, while I was on a conference call, no less, and put her foot down. She said that either she sees you at Christmas dinner, or it's the last I see of her."

He picks up his wine glass, swirls it around, and brings it to his lips. "She is a ruthless negotiator. I didn't stand a chance."

I look from Stonehart to Rose without understanding. What is the basis of their relationship? Stonehart *cannot* be merely an employer. There has to be something more.

Charles smiles at our exchange and takes Rose's hand again. Where does he fit in, for that matter?

After we have finished the appetizers, Charles gets up and brings out the single largest turkey I've ever seen. It's golden brown outside, with red cranberry stuffing falling out of the inside.

Charles looks at it with pride as he sets it down.

He makes a series of rapid hand motions that Stonehart translates for me.

"He says that he made it especially for you."

I blink, startled. A tiny sliver of hope comes to life inside me.

*Charles made the turkey for me. Rose threatened to resign because of me.*

Maybe things aren't quite as bleak as they seem.

***

Dinner continues with flowing drinks and delicious turkey. Rose and Stonehart chat like old friends, while Charles signs his comments to both of them. Stonehart has the presence of mind to translate for me.

Other than that, though, I try to stay unnoticed. I have nothing to say to Stonehart—not in front of company.

And yet, halfway through dinner, I find myself caught in the currents of conversation. The wine is exerting its effect on me. My reservation is slowly being replaced by a curious excitement that comes from nothing more than being around people again.

I wonder how or why Stonehart learned sign language. Was it just for Charles's benefit?

I decide to ask him.

He blinks when he hears my question. The joy seeps out of his face.

"My mother lost her hearing when I was ten," he says. For half a second, he looks surprised to have told me. Then his eyes darken. He looks me up and down, as if seeing me for the first time.

Or – a tingle of fear creeps up my spine – as if just remembering who I really am.

Rose catches the exchange, and rescues me in time. "So, Lilly," she asks breezily, "have you given any thought to what you're going to do on your trip?"

"Trip?" I ask. "What trip?"

"Oops." Rose brings a hand over her mouth. But her eyes are dancing, and she doesn't sound the least bit guilty.

Stonehart clears his throat. "The trip," he emphasizes, "that Lilly was not supposed to know about until tomorrow morning."

"Looks like the cat's out of the bag," Rose smiles at him, taking a sip of wine.

"So it does," Stonehart agrees. I don't hear

displeasure or annoyance in his voice. Maybe a slight hint of irritation — maybe — but that is probably better attributed to my own nerves after the near-miss.

"What trip?" I ask again, turning toward Stonehart.

"It was supposed to be your Christmas surprise," he says.

"Oh, don't pout, Jeremy," Rose chastises. "It's not a good look for you."

My eyes fly to her, wide in shock. Did she just *reprimand* Stonehart? Not only that, but she *also* called him by his first name?

*Unbelievable.*

Stonehart seems just as surprised by what he heard as I am. But he covers it up quickly, and gives a rich laugh.

"You're right, Rose," he says. "As always, you're right. What I would do without you, I don't know."

She sidles up taller in her chair, proud as a mother hen.

Stonehart takes my hand. My breath catches in my throat — it's the first time he's touched me since saying grace. I guess part of my reaction is the ingrained apprehension that grew from all those nights spent in the dark.

"Tomorrow," he says softly, looking me deep in the eyes, "I have a business trip planned to Portland. I will be busy most of the day, but I've made arrangements for you to join me. Rose helped me prepare certain activities that she tells me you will find most satisfying." He glances at her, and she smiles back at him.

"That is," he continues after a moment, "if you're

willing to go with me."

My mind reels in disbelief and wonder. A trip? Off the estate? To *Portland*?

And — most impressive of all — he's asking me? Not telling, but actually *asking*?

*What's the catch?* I wonder.

I lick my lips before answering. Rose is watching me with a hopeful expression on her face. Charles is smiling broadly. And Stonehart?

Well, Stonehart is looking at me in a way that reminds me of a boy asking a girl out on a date for the first time. Expectation mingles with uncertainty over his features. It's such a soft, endearing look — and so far away from what I've come to expect from him — that it has me saying, before I can think, "Jeremy, of course I'll go with you. I'd love to."

A great smile splits his face. He claps his hands together. The noise startles us back into the present moment.

"Wonderful," he says. "Simply wonderful." He leans over and kisses my cheek. "Rose, you devil, you knew how nervous I was about asking her, and you forced my hand anyway."

Rose gives a slight, self-satisfied smile, half-hidden by her wineglass. "It's what I do best."

# Chapter Five

With the safety afforded by Charles' and Rose's company, the rest of the night goes by in a cocktail of joviality and drinking and mirth.

I don't remember the last time I felt so carefree. A large part of it is the wine warming my belly.

After dinner, the four of us move from room to room in the enormous mansion. There's music playing from hidden speakers in the walls. Stonehart shows me the massive Christmas tree he had erected on the main floor. It reaches all the way to the ceiling and sparkles with hundreds of little lights. I've never seen one so large before.

At some indeterminate point, Rose and Charles sneak off. I only realize they're gone when it's just me and Stonehart in the room.

My gut tightens in immediate apprehension. This is the moment I've been dreading all night.

Stonehart, who was about to sit beside me, senses my stiffness and backs off. He strides to the opposite wall and looks at his reflection in the dark glass.

"So," he finally exhales, turning to me, "I trust you had a good time tonight?"

I nod, maintaining appearances. I need to be polite.

"I enjoyed myself, too," he tells me. He seems to be struggling with something. His jaw works as his eyes look me over.

I sit stiff as a statue.

"Listen, Lilly, I—" he cuts off, clamps his mouth shut. A moment later, he tries again.

"I—I don't want you to despise me. I know it's a

stretch. But I still hold out hope that it's not too late."

Alarm bells go off in my head. My nails dig deep into the armrest.

He sighs again. "It's not often I admit that I'm wrong," he says. "It's not often that I *am* wrong. But I'm starting to think that I was, with you."

I try to remain passive, but his words spark a sudden attentiveness in me.

"It's your strength that astounds me," he continues when I don't speak. His back is still toward me, but I can see his expression against the window. It looks pained, conflicted. Torn. "When I first brought you here, not once did I think that you would hold out for so long. I did not intend for you to suffer for so long."

He gives a mirthless chuckle and glances back at me. Our eyes meet for a split second. His dart away first.

"I know you've suffered, Lilly. I watched you in that room. I saw you through the cameras. When I presented you with the contract, I thought that you would sign it in a matter of days. 'A week, tops,' I told myself. 'There is no way she will hold out for more.'

"But you surprised both of us. You remained there, firm in your resolve, for six weeks. *Six weeks.* That's nearly two months, Lilly. That was... unbelievable."

He trails off. I don't dare move. This is the closest we've ever come to discussing my... imprisonment.

I can't interrupt. Not now.

"Your continuous act of defiance made me realize how strong you really were. And then, when you told Rose my name, before I made it known I was holding you here—well, that was also something that left a great impression on me."

He turns to a liquor cabinet. He takes a tumbler out and pours himself a splash of scotch. He offers the bottle to me.

I shake my head, afraid that a single word on my part will break the confession.

He shrugs, tips the scotch back, and downs it in one swallow. Then he drops in two fresh ice cubes. He pours some more liquor in, this time swirling the glass until the ice clinks against the sides.

He walks toward me, but does not sit at my side. Instead, he takes the seat across the coffee table

He drops his head back to look up at the tall ceiling.

"I knew you would be tough to break," he

continues finally. "That is why I treated you so harshly. The TGBs, my expectations, the rules, the way I presented myself to you — all of it was to teach you that I was in control. I had to make you ready for the things I had planned for you."

"What sort of things?" I ask softly, not knowing if I even want to hear the answer.

"Great things." He looks at me and smiles. "Great things, Lilly. Opportunities that you cannot even imagine. The Dextran offer was just a start."

"You mean — that's actually *real*?" I ask. I know I expressed my incredulity before, many times, but Stonehart is in a mood I've never seen before. An *indulgent* mood.

"Yes," he says. He stands up. I've never seen it this difficult for him to keep still.

"When you met Esteban — you remember that

day, don't you? I thought we were making progress, you and I. I thought—and forgive me for being so blunt—that there was a trust developing between us. It was what I hoped for."

I stare at him struck dumb. *He* hoped for *trust*? *He* wanted *trust*, when, no matter what happened, my whole life was under his control?

*How much more "trust" does the man need?*

"Much more," Stonehart says. My hands fly over my mouth when I realize that I had actually spoken that last thought out loud.

"I wanted the trust that a young woman gives to the love of her life. The trust that husband and wife share after fifty years together. The trust that comforts you and keeps you safe, even when you are in the darkest places of this world."

I don't need to do anything to express my

immense disbelief. Stonehart tells me exactly what he thinks with a loud scoff.

"Of course, I knew that we were not there. I knew that we might never get there. But that did not stop me from holding out *hope*, Lilly, that one day, we might. I saw that things were changing.

"And then, a few nights later, you caught me with... *Angelica*." He whispers her name. "I became furious. Not at you — at myself. I was livid for being so careless, for being so tactless, for being so fucking weak. I did not need *her* when I had you."

He chuckles again, though this time it sounds forced. "But old habits die hard, I guess. What's that saying about an old dog? No new tricks? And I'm no stranger to the passage of time.

"I knew it was you as soon as I heard the noise outside the window. Who else could it be? And when I came to your room and found you tucked in your bed, I knew that you were trying to deceive me. Trying to *trick* me."

A growl comes from his throat. I shift uncomfortably under his suddenly-hard stare. "That did not make me happy. I tried to contain my rage, but I knew that if I pretended not to know what you did, it would make both of us look like fools. Still — still! — I almost walked away. I was halfway out of the room when I noticed your footprints on the floor. At that point, I had no choice but to punish you. I could not ignore them.

"But you remember what I said next, don't you? That, from that moment on, every time I see you, I wanted you on your hands and knees? I regretted those words. The next morning, when I left, I spent the whole day wishing I could take them back. That's why, when I returned, I did not raise qualms about your non-compliance."

"You ignored me," I say.

"I was trying to save face," he sighs. "I could not have you see me waver in my demands. That would make me seem weak. And I hate weakness above all."

"It would make you seem *human*," I whisper.

He grunts. "Perhaps. But I was not ready to show you that side of me then." He turns, faces me, and walks straight forward. His eyes bore into me as he advances. I don't shy away, no matter how much I want to.

What he does next takes me completely by surprise. He *drops to his knees*, and picks up my hand. "But I am now," he whispers.

I blink through suddenly-moist eyes. Am I crying?

Why? I've never been overly weepy before…

But listening to Stonehart speak has all sorts of strange emotions bubbling up inside of me. Seeing him on his knees like that has me absolutely awe-struck.

"You can ask me anything you want," he says into my hand. "Just let me finish my story first."

I nod dumbly, hardly able to reconcile what is happening with the Stonehart I know.

He gets back up and starts to pace the room again. "The two weeks away felt like the longest of my life. The goddamned trip had to happen at the moment we were making the most progress. I worried the entire time that when I returned, we would have regressed.

"But that was not the only thing troubling me. It took me less than a day to begin missing you.

Somehow, at one point or another, you became my drug. I became addicted to you, Lilly. I needed my fix.

"I was not myself the entire trip. I made poor decisions. Bad judgments. Even my colleagues commented on it. All because I could not get you out of my mind.

"Half a dozen times I debated flying home to see you. Half a dozen times I wanted to fly straight back just to hold you in my arms. No other woman has ever had such a strong effect on me."

I stare at him in disbelief. I don't know what to say.

"When my plane landed in California that day, my composure disappeared. I had waited so long to see you. All pretense was gone. I rushed home, my heart racing, ready to apologize for the way I'd been treating you, for the things I'd been doing to you, ready to confess all my budding feelings for you, only to find you—"

"Asleep," I whisper.

"Yes," he says. "Asleep."

A silence forms between us. It is not comfortable.

After a minute, Stonehart speaks again.

"You cannot imagine the disappointment I felt. Finding you like that told me the feelings I harbored for you were one-sided. I felt powerless. It was all an illusion. There was no reciprocity. You did not want to see me."

I swallow. Is this the insight into Stonehart's mind that I always wanted?

"I thought maybe you would wake. I thought that maybe, I should wait. But as I did… and as the minutes stretched… a deep fury rose inside of me. I was angered at my own weakness. At the feelings for you that were growing inside me.

"I was wrong. Nothing had changed. Even worse. After two weeks away, we'd *regressed*, just as I feared.

"I did not want to lose you. But I felt like you were slipping out of my fingertips. So I did the only thing I could, Lilly. I exerted control. I had to, Lilly, don't you see? I *had* to do it. I had to. You gave me no choice. I had to—" he looks away from me then, "—I had to leave you in the dark."

He clears his throat. His next words come out in a harsh whisper. "When you're in the dark, with your collar on, I know that you are safe."

He holds up a hand to stop my protest before I can give it voice. "I know what that sounds like. I shudder to think what type of monster that makes me in your eyes. I know I've been less than kind to you, Lilly. You deserve better. Better than what I've given you. But some things…" he exhales heavily, "…some things go so much further back than you can ever know."

He sits up and faces me. "So there you have it. It's a goddamn horrible apology, but it's the only one I can give you now."

Our eyes meet. Behind the darkness that engulfs his irises, I see a tumultuous swirling of emotions.

I wonder if the same is mirrored in my face. Because, this… this *confession*… has me reeling.

He rises. "Our flight leaves tomorrow at ten," he says. "Rose will be in to wake you before eight. She'll pack your belongings for you."

He walks to me and reaches out to take my hand.

I don't move. I feel like I'm glued to the spot.

He brings my knuckles to his lips. "Goodnight, Lilly-flower," he breathes. "And Merry Christmas. I hope, starting tomorrow, we can begin a new chapter in our lives."

Without another word, he turns around and walks out the room, leaving me feeling like I've just been run over by a ten-ton truck.

# Chapter Six

My mind is too active to grant me any sleep that night.

I keep replaying the conversation with Stonehart over and over again in my head. Three things stand out:

The first is his plea not to hate him. I never, ever would have thought I would hear anything of the sort from the man.

The second is the mention of hope. He *hopes* that I can trust him. He *hopes* that he can trust me.

The third is the promise of a new chapter. What does he mean by that? Have the rules been abolished? He's taking me out with him, with no mention of the TGBs. Are they nothing more than a relic now?

He also told me that I can ask him questions. Any I like! I didn't seize the opportunity before he left. But, if he actually stays true to his word, it might mean that the verbal rules he set out at our first meeting do not apply anymore.

I turn to my side and bring the blanket to cover my shoulder. I stare out at the sea. Moonlight reflects off the glassy water and makes it seem to sparkle.

I cannot wrap my mind around what could have possessed Stonehart to say all those things to me. It's the closest thing to empathetic I've ever seen him.

I do not think he was mincing words. Why would he? The justifications he had for his actions make little enough sense as they were.

Little enough sense to someone *normal*. He imprisoned me to keep me *safe*? He locked me up to develop *trust*?

That is not how those things work.

One other thing he said, just before walking out the room, has me more confused and uncertain than ever.

*"Some things go so much further back than you can ever know."*

Was he alluding to the reason I'm here? To the reason why I was the one he chose as his prisoner?

I can't be sure. But I know one thing: Whatever he meant, it was important. The sincerity he showed in giving that twisted explanation for his actions tells me, without a shadow of a doubt, that I am important to him.

I suspect I was important before I even came to California.

*Why?* and *How?* are the prevailing questions that haunt me as I drift off into a restless sleep.

***

Bleary-eyed and groggy, I wake up the next morning to Rose shaking my arm.

"Miss Ryder, it's time to get up," she says in an apologetic, soft voice.

I groan and roll onto my back. It feels like I just fell asleep minutes ago.

"Miss Ryder, you really can't wait any longer. It's almost nine-thirty, and —"

I jerk upright, more awake than if I had chugged five Red Bulls in a row.

"The flight's at ten!" I gasp. "Jeremy said you'd

wake me at eight, and—"

"Shh, shh, it's okay," Rose breaks in, cutting me off. "Mr. Stonehart saw how soundly you were sleeping and wanted to give you a little more time to rest. You'll be taking a separate flight to Portland, leaving at noon."

Relief swells inside, mixed with a hint of disbelief. Stonehart changes plans because of *me*?

"But you really mustn't tarry," Rose says. "We're cutting it close. If you want, you can take a quick shower. I have everything packed for you."

I let Rose lead me out of bed. I slip a robe over my shoulders as she chatters on. Even though she's trying hard to retain the degree of formality that defined our very first conversations, she can't keep some things from slipping out.

"It's wonderful to be able to see you again," she

keeps telling me. "Oh, and I'm so excited for your trip. I hear Portland isn't the grandest of cities, but I've never been, and it's beyond time you get out of the house..."

On and on she goes, in that same, bubbly vein, as I get dressed and then sip the espresso she brings me.

"Oh my God!" I exclaim as the first bit of caffeine hits my bloodstream. "It's Christmas! I forgot all about it, Rose. Merry Christmas."

"And to you too, dear,' she says with a coy smile.

"I don't have anything to give you," I admit. Even though I never had much money, I always made a point of putting some small gifts together for my friends during the holidays. Most of them were useless knick-knacks, but they were always appreciated. I wish I had something for Rose.

She smiles at me in a very endearing way. "Just

seeing you healthy and happy is enough for me," she says. Then she claps her hands together. "Now, come along, please. I've got your luggage lined up for you at the front, and the limo's waiting. The driver's been idling—"

"Hold on," I say, stopping short. "Where's Jeremy?"

"Mr. Stonehart took the ten a.m. flight as planned," Rose tells me. "He arranged for his plane to return to bring you to Portland this afternoon."

My eyebrows rise in surprise. So he really did have to get there early. And still, he left me here on my own, just to give me a few extra hours of sleep?

"That was very considerate of him," I mumble.

"Mr. Stonehart can be a considerate man," Rose beams proudly. She touches my shoulder. "He just has to have the right people around to bring it out."

***

Half an hour later, I'm seated in the back of a
white limousine, about to leave Stonehart's property
for the first time.

A nervous excitement fills me as the engine starts
up and the car rolls off. I wave goodbye to Rose
through the back window, and, when the mansion is
out of sight, stick my face to the glass to look at the
winding road we're taking through the trees.

The gates rise in front of us soon after. They are
large and heavy and black. Very, very black.

Seeing those gates makes my hand twitch up to
touch the collar around my neck.

It's still there, of course. But I've become so

accustomed to its presence that I rarely notice it any more. And right now, in some strange yet undeniable way, it feels… almost soothing.

It lets me know that I am not dreaming. It tells me that I really *am* about to leave Stonehart's property, having earned the promised TGBs or not.

The gate slides open. My breath hitches as we drive through. And then, when nothing happens… I let out a strangled laugh of relief.

The driver glances at me through the rearview mirror as my laughter becomes near-hysterical. I don't care. I am off the property. I am actually *off* the property.

There was no shock. There was no pain. The collar remained deactivated, true to Stonehart's word.

I couldn't be happier.

Two days ago, I was trapped in the dark, unsure of whether or not I'd ever see the light of day again. And now, here I am, in the back of a limousine, about to enter the busy California traffic, as close to a free woman as I've ever dared hope.

Half an hour later, we arrive at a private airfield. There's a small jet waiting nearby. A stewardess takes my bags from the trunk and carries them on board with the driver's help. I climb the protruding steps to the cabin and look around.

It's as luxurious as I imagined. More so. The seats bolted to the floor are a rich, creamy red. A bar made of dark oak is installed near the back. There's a second stewardess behind the counter. She smiles at me when our eyes meet.

"Good morning, Miss Ryder," she announces in a crisp, upbeat voice. "Would you like anything to drink?"

She knows my name? Then again, of course she would. Stonehart would have ensured that.

I eye the fancy bottles behind her. My head throbs a little from the wine last night. Besides, I want to be fully sober when I see Stonehart in a few hours.

"Just water, thank you," I say, and pick a seat at random to perch on. She brings me my glass and I take it with a grateful smile, but don't bring it to my lips.

Being all alone — that is, without Stonehart — in this place feels surreal. More than that, it feels like I'm *intruding*. I don't belong in places usually reserved for the rich and famous. I don't belong in the cabin of a magnificent private jet.

The stewardess from outside climbs the stairs and seals the door. The plane taxis to the runway, and we're lifting off a few minutes later.

I'm not afraid of heights, but I've never been a big fan of flying. My body tenses as the elevation changes. I relax only when we're level high in the air.

The flight to Portland passes in the blink of an eye. I spend most my time staring out the little circular window. I don't see anything but white clouds. Yet, something about what they represent—the promise of real, genuine freedom—appeals to the deepest part of me.

"The wind is in our favor," one of the attendants tells me. "We're going to arrive half an hour early." She smiles, as if it's the greatest news in the world.

We land. The touchdown is a little bumpy, but, on the whole, better than lift off. The doors open and I'm hit by a frigid blast of air.

Now, I'm thankful for the coat Rose stuffed in my

hands before I left.

I drape it over my shoulders and descend the steps. My bags are already being loaded into a black limousine that's waiting for me. This one is shorter than the last. I never gave such things much thought before. But, I guess limos come in different sizes.

The driver is a plain-faced man with gray streaks in his hair. He holds the door open for me. I thank him with a little nod, and, happy to get out of the cold, duck inside.

Surprise overcomes me when I find Stonehart lounging on the other side of the cabin, his cell phone pressed to one ear.

He's leaning back with one arm draped over the back of the seat. He is the picture of masculine ease.

Our eyes meet. He smiles at me briefly, and then looks away as he continues his conversation. The door slams closed behind me, making me jump. Stonehart notices, and a spark of amusement flickers across his eyes.

I settle directly across from him, wishing there was a little more room in the tight cabin. *I thought he had meetings to attend today*, I think. *Yet, he made time to meet me.*

The car starts to move. I feign interest in the passing scenery outside, but in truth, nothing could be more interesting than listening in on Stonehart's conversation. He's talking business, something about shorting stocks. While I have no idea of the context, anything he says that has to do with Stonehart Industries is fascinating to me.

Any tidbit I overhear now might prove vital in the future.

*Escape*, I think in the back of my mind. *I made it out*

*of the mansion. The next step is to get away from him.*

The phone call ends unfortunately early. Stonehart hangs up only minutes after we leave the airport.

"I'm sorry about that," he says. "Your flight came early. That was rude of me."

I give a little laugh. I'm not sure if it comes from a genuine place or if I do it just to play the role I think Stonehart expects of me. "Don't worry about it. Honestly."

But my spirits are higher than they have been in weeks. That's no act. And it's pretty obvious as to why.

"You had a good flight?" Stonehart asks. "Did Charlene give you any trouble?"

"Charlene?" I wrinkle my nose. "Who's

Charlene?"

"My pilot," Stonehart says, looking momentarily confused. "She didn't introduce herself?"

I shake my head. "No." I look at him. "You have a *female* pilot?"

He answers me with a rich laugh. "Is that so hard to believe?"

"I guess not," I say. "Just… somewhat against the usual stereotype."

"True," Stonehart concedes.

"Thank you for letting me sleep in, by the way," I say. "I told Rose it was very considerate of you."

He perks an eyebrow. "And what did Rose have to say to that?"

"She said you can be a considerate man." I pause, debating whether or not to add the other part. I decide to do it. "For the right people."

"And you, my dear, definitely belong to that select group," he says, with no hint or mockery or sarcasm in his voice.

I can't help the smile that grows on my lips.

"But I must apologize," Stonehart continues. "We're almost at our hotel, and I do have meetings to attend. I wanted to greet you. Beyond that, I'm afraid we won't be able to spend much time together today. Before we part, however, I wanted to go over my rules for this trip."

My heart sinks. I knew this was coming, but I was hoping he would delay it for a tiny bit longer. It jars me from the illusion of freedom I'd built up around this trip and right back into harsh reality.

"But first," he says, reaching into his coat pocket, "a gift. For you. It is Christmas, after all."

He brings out a small black box and holds it in front of him. It's the sort that would house an expensive ring or bracelet.

*Oh God.* I swallow. I hope this isn't a return of the TGBs.

"Open it, Lilly," he says.

I take it from his outstretched hand. The box has surprising weight. It's solidly built.

I feel Stonehart's eyes focus on me. Something shifts in the air, and there's a sudden solemnity between us. I try not to show my growing nerves. After a moment's hesitation, I lift the top.

Inside is a beautiful, jeweled brooch in the shape of a butterfly. The wings are made of red rubies and green emeralds. The body is a shiny silver or platinum.

"Christmas colors," Stonehart says. "I thought they would suit you for the holidays."

I hold my breath. He hasn't mentioned this being a TGB yet. Maybe there isn't any hidden meaning behind the gift.

"Here," Stonehart says. "Let me put it on."

I turn the box to him and let him take the butterfly out. He leans forward. His hands move sure and swift as he unbuttons my jacket to expose the blouse I have on underneath. My breath hitches as he spreads the lapels wide and focuses on my chest. Slowly, he pins the brooch in place.

An intense sexual energy cackles between our bodies. I have the overwhelming urge to kiss him.

Before I can make good on that foolish desire, Stonehart leans back, breaking me from the trance. He smiles.

"It looks good on you, Lilly-flower," he says softly.

"Thank you, Jeremy," I answer, my words coming out a touch breathless.

"You're welcome," he says. He lifts a finger. "Now, rule number one. You are to keep the brooch on at all times during our trip."

Alarm ripples down my back. I knew there was a trap here somewhere. He wouldn't make such a rule if it didn't hold meaning.

"Why?" I ask, even though I do not want to know the answer.

"Because," Stonehart smiles, "located inside is a small positioning chip. It transmits a signal to your collar," He takes out his phone, swipes at the screen, and then leans back in apparent satisfaction. "Which is active as of this moment. So long as the brooch remains within three feet of you, you're free to go wherever you please. But the moment you step out of range…?" he trails off. "I don't think I need to finish for you to understand."

Anger and frustration build inside me. I take a series of deep, steadying breaths to quell those feelings.

*Really Lilly,* I tell myself. *This isn't so bad. Did you really expect Stonehart to just let you roam around Portland with no restrictions?*

I force a smile that I hope he takes as genuine. I am his prisoner once more. Then again — that never really changed.

"Okay," I say. "The brooch stays on. What else?"

Stonehart's eyebrows come up. "That's it? No protest? No indignation?"

I shrug as casually as I can. "Nope."

He gives a little smirk. "Good. I'm glad we've progressed past that. Though, I fear you might be a little more opposed to the bit of information that comes next."

I look right at him with my back straight. "Shoot."

"The reason you need to keep the brooch on, sweet Lilly, is because there is a microphone embedded inside. It's been recording everything that's been said since the moment you opened the box. Every word you say on this trip... everything you hear..." he taps his earpiece, "I do, too." He pauses to gauge my reaction and then continues.

"It's just a precaution, you see. I am granting you unparalleled freedom, and I simply do not want you tempted into making some very, very dangerous decisions." His eyes bore into me as his voice

103

becomes dark. "Do you understand the things I am talking about, Lilly?"

I shift a little under that stare. I understand all too well. He wouldn't want me going to the cops or calling for help.

"Remember that, ultimately, I control your collar," he says. "If the wrong words come from those pretty red lips of yours, all it takes is one press of a button…" He holds up his phone to show me. "…and you're writhing on the floor."

Bile builds in my throat at the casual way he can speak of electrocuting me.

His voice softens a fraction. "But I don't want you worried about that during this trip. I want you to enjoy yourself. Just use your common sense, Lilly, and we'll avoid any accidents.

"Now, obviously, I don't have the time nor the

inclination to listen in on your every word today, or tomorrow, or any other day this trip. That's why the task has been relegated to Rose." His eyes move up to meet mine. "I assure you," he says softly, "you do not want to test her loyalty to me. If you do…" He pauses. "The result will be very unpleasant. For both of you."

I clear my throat and look out the window. Rose will be the one spying on me? Well, things could certainly be worse.

Although, I guess that in a way, that limits what I can do, knowing Rose will bear the brunt of the blame if anything goes wrong is a stronger deterrent than the collar itself.

I turn back to him. "I understand, Jeremy. Thank you for informing me of your — " I stall. " — Precautions."

"Of course," he says. "You must know the parameters governing your behavior for this trip if you are expected to remain within them." He reaches out to take my hand. I stop myself from recoiling just as his fingers brush over mine. "Don't do anything that would displease me, and this trip can be quite prosperous for both of us."

With that, he opens the door, and steps out onto the busy downtown street in front of a spiraling steel and glass tower.

"You'll be brought to the hotel, where you will remain until evening. If you prefer, I've given permission to the driver to chauffer you around the city. You're not to leave the car, but that doesn't mean you can't do some sightseeing from the back."

# Chapter Seven

The thrill of being in a new city is somewhat diminished by the fact that I can experience it only from the back of a vehicle.

Still, I have little reason to complain. Stonehart went over the rules without being overtly unpleasant. Even if I don't like them very much, I understand the need to establish boundaries beforehand. Initial parameters are essential to ensure compliance of both parties in the agreement.

*Jesus.* I stop short. I'm starting to sound like Stonehart!

*Focus, Lilly. Think!* I tell myself. *You're out of the mansion. Look for an escape!*

But is escape even possible now? The collar is still

around my neck. The brooch has a GPS chip so that Stonehart can track me wherever I go. I look at the door handle. Undoubtedly, it's locked. I can't just plunge out of the car into city traffic.

And even if I could… what would I do then? The collar would send me thrashing to the ground in moments. It would cause a scene in public. For any onlooker it would look like I'm having a seizure. I'd pass out. Somebody would probably call the paramedics. Then I'd wake up in a hospital wing somewhere, safe and far away…

No. Not safe. Not far away. Stonehart would find me. He would be furious. I've seen the extent of his anger.

I sigh and settle back. I cannot run yet. I need to bide my time and wait for the perfect opportunity. I cannot do it blind.

Besides, I want more than to simply escape. I want to get back at Stonehart for everything he's done to me. I *need* to get back at Stonehart for everything he's done to me. To have the opportunity, I need to stay close to him.

I spend the next hour or so directing the driver through the streets. Portland is quite small for a major city. It has a certain antiquity that I imagine would be quite charming… if I could experience it from outside the car.

In time, I get bored of sitting in the back. I want to stretch my legs. I ask the driver to bring me to the hotel.

It takes ten minutes to get there. My mind wanders to the conversation Stonehart and I had last night. It was the most honest I've ever seen him.

Or maybe not. It's difficult to tell when the man is

being honest. He *sounded* sincere, sure, but maybe the entire thing was another attempt at manipulation.

We arrive at the hotel. It's an upscale place — obviously. In the garage, the driver takes my bags and leads me to a private elevator sheltered behind a locked gate.

He enters with me without a word. He hits the topmost button on the panel after inserting a small key. The elevator shoots up.

The doors open to a magnificent penthouse suite. The driver places my bags over the threshold and tips his cap. "Enjoy your stay, Miss Ryder," he says, and then vanishes behind the closing doors.

I wait without moving for a count of sixty. Then I turn around and try to call the lift up by myself.

No such luck. The light remains off. The elevator is the only way in or out of the suite. It looks like I'm to remain here until Stonehart arrives.

I turn back and look at the new space. The décor is a departure from what I've gotten used to in Stonehart's mansion. Instead of sleek minimalism, it's more elaborate and showy. Expensive paintings hang on the walls. The light fixtures above me are gilded. The cold, tile floor is covered by expensive Persian rugs.

I walk through the suite to get a sense of its size. It's *massive*. Immense. It doesn't just take up the entire story of the hotel. It takes up two. An open floor plan on the second level allows me to see the bedrooms from the living room floor.

I yawn as I pass one luxurious-looking bed. I glance at the clock on the wall. It shows a few minutes after four. Stonehart is bound to be working for a few more hours, yet. And I didn't get a complete night's sleep.

I lower myself onto the bed and sigh in relief as my body hits the soft mattress. I check on the brooch to make sure it's in no danger of falling off. Next, I pick up one corner of the blanket, fling it over me, and close my eyes, drifting off into a peaceful sleep.

\*\*\*

Something vague and uncertain tugs me from sleep. I open my eyes, and find Stonehart leaning against the doorway in the bedroom.

My breath hitches in alarm. I remember what happened last time he found me like this. I start to scramble up, but Stonehart stops me with a calming gesture.

"Lie still," he says. "Relax. I only just got here. You're in no danger of displeasing me."

He walks toward the bed and sits by my legs. His crisp suit accents his body shape and makes him look stunning.

He places a hand above my knee, on my inner thigh. Even through the fabric I can feel the warmth of his touch.

His eyes trail up my body. His thumb moves back and forth against my leg. He meets my eyes. I see what must be one of his rare genuine smiles.

"Hi," he says softly. "How are you?"

"I'm…good," I say after a moment, my mind still a little fuzzy from sleep.

"I have a question for you," Stonehart says. He takes my hand. "And it is my most genuine hope that you say *yes*."

A shudder runs through me as he brings my hand to his lips and kisses my palm. He lets go, but I keep my hand there, brushing the short stubble on his jaw.

*Is this a dream?* I wonder. *Am I still sleeping?*

"What is it?" My words come soft, matching his. The melody of our voices lends an ethereal aura to the bedroom.

"Would you be interested," he begins, a small glimmer showing in his eyes, "In accompanying me to dinner tonight?"

"Where?" I ask.

Stonehart smiles. "Not here, obviously. Outside. In public. At a magnificent restaurant overlooking the Columbia River.

I push myself up and look at him. "You're

actually serious?"

He gives me a lazy smile. "Of course I am, sweet Lily." He rubs my leg in a slow, unhurried way. "The reservation is set. All that's required is your approval."

"Then yes," I say, hardly believing this conversation. "Yes! I'd love to go to dinner with you tonight, Jeremy."

He nods. "Good," he says. He looks like he's on the verge of saying more, but then he gives a miniscule shake of his head and stands. "I'll give you an hour to get ready. Is that enough time?"

"Too much," I say. "I don't need an hour. Just let me fix my hair and I'll be ready in —"

"Lilly." Stonehart holds up one hand and stops me short. His voice is firm but gentle. "I told you there's no rush. Take the hour. Have a shower. You don't need to be on edge with me. Not tonight."

He turns back and starts out of the room.

"Wait," I call after him. "Are there going to be…
rules?"

He misses a step. When he speaks, he doesn't look
at me, instead staring straight ahead. " 'Rules,'" he
quotes. "Yes, Lilly, there are going to be rules. I was
hoping to inform you of them on the drive there."

He glances over his shoulder. "I don't want such
things troubling you yet."

"I think now would be—"

"No, Lilly!" This time he snaps the command. "I
said I'll tell you of them later, and that's what I
intend to do. Don't question me on such things."

"Okay," I whisper. I don't want to provoke him,
not when I can tell he's trying so hard to stay in

control. "Um, Jeremy? When I shower, the brooch…?"

"It was deactivated the minute you stepped into this suite. Along with the collar. When you're in here, you don't need to worry about holding your tongue. It's not like there's anybody you can talk to." He turns and faces me. "For future reference: any residences you visit with me, that are mine, will work with the brooch and collar the same way."

"You mean…" I narrow my eyes slightly, half from disbelief, "…that you intend to bring me to other places?"

"Provided your behavior outside my San Jose mansion continues to be exemplary," he pauses. "Then yes. There's a whole world out there that I have built to my image. It would be a dastardly shame to be unable to share it with you. I want you at my side, Lilly-flower, and I want to show you the wonders that Stonehart Industries has granted me. I own property worldwide: Resorts, other mansions, beautiful villas. They have seen infrequent use. I've been waiting for something… someone… to share that with."

"Me?" I say, almost certain that this is another jest, just like the Dextran job.

"Yes, my dear. You." He chuckles. "You mustn't look so surprised. You didn't truly think I'd keep you locked away forever. How could I? You're so beautiful, so precious. Your radiance demands to be shared with the world. I've attended galas and events with dozens of stunning women. Yet none of them have ever held a candle to you." He touches his chest. "Not in my heart."

With that, he turns away again. "An hour, Lilly.

Starting right now. But please," he takes a deep, controlled breath. "Don't be late."

***

Forty minutes later, I'm fresh out the shower and dressed in a magnificent, black silk dress. The neckline is embedded with tiny, clear, precious stones. I suspect they're diamonds. I mean, why wouldn't they be? But I have no experience with such things to be sure.

The brooch is fastened on my left shoulder strap. It adds a splash of color that complements my appearance quite nicely. If it wasn't for what it represents…

No. I stop myself from going down that path of

thoughts. I wanted to get close to Stonehart. This trip — this dinner — will be my first real chance to do so in weeks.

Can I pretend my last stint in the dark never occurred? No. Of course not. What Stonehart did to me there… the horrible way he made me feel… none of it can ever be forgotten. But I cannot show that I bear him any ill will. This trip to Portland, the dinner tonight — in public! — is the first tangible step I've made with him probably ever. This is real progress.

And yet… I can't stop feeling that something is not right. It's almost like Stonehart is trying to lure me into a false sense of security just before pulling the rug out from under my feet.

I suppress a shudder. I desperately hope that's not the case. And I know that worrying about it will lead me nowhere. I need to stay on my guard, remain cautious… and not do anything to provoke another punishment from Stonehart.

I enter the foyer and find him reclining in a grand armchair, looking out at the darkening city skyline. He'd changed into a pristine black tuxedo while I was showering.

I stop, and for a second or two simply look at the man. He hasn't noticed me yet. I think this might be the first time that I have been able to look at Stonehart without him knowing I'm there.

He looks… damn good. One of his hands is idly tugging at a cufflink on his other wrist. His facial profile is so prefect it would make a sculptor weep. Everything from the angular jaw, to the prominent nose, to the deep-set yet beautiful eyes, makes him an image of utter male splendor.

And right now, he's unguarded. This is a rare

122

glimpse of Stonehart when he thinks he's alone.

Somehow, that makes all the things he's responsible for secondary to his sheer presence. There's no pretense with him right now. No masks. I don't have to dissemble who he is or what he wants. What I see is what I get: Jeremy Stonehart, raw and unadulterated.

"Are you going to stare at me forever," he says without moving his gaze from the window, "Or are you going to give some indication that you're there?"

He turns his head, then, and his eyes bore into me. There's a heated intensity contained there.

Panic rises within me. That type of look has only meant one thing in the past: That I've done something wrong.

Before I can move or say a word, Stonehart is out of the chair and looming before me. I brace myself for something—what, I don't know—but what I get instead surpasses every expectation.

Stonehart puts one hand above my hip, tugs me into him, and kisses me fiercely.

The kiss is a mixture of molten lava and smoldering passion. He hasn't ever kissed me like this. No one has.

Heat flows into me and the blood drains from my head as my body responds to him in the most natural way possible. Stonehart's kiss consumes me. I let it do so entirely.

When he finally lets go, my legs are shaky. My lips are swollen from the assault. And I can feel heat—palpable, scorching heat—radiating from my cheeks and neck and chest.

I'd mistaken the look in his eyes. It wasn't displeasure. It was *desire*.

How I am able to prompt such passion in him, I will never know.

Or why my body still responds to him this way, after all that he's put me through.

"I've been wanting to do that for a very long time," he growls. His voice is low and husky. "And when I saw you walk out, I couldn't wait any longer."

He touches the side of my face. His thumb leaves a scorching line down my cheek as it wonders to the corner of my lips. "Forgive my... impropriety."

"It's forgiven," I say, breathless and still reeling.

*This is the same man who starved you!* A tiny voice screams at me. *This is the same man who —*

I shut it up ruthlessly. I know who Stonehart is. I know what he's done to me, and all that he's responsible for. Those are not things one can forget. But when he kisses me like this… when he makes me feel so deliciously turned on, against all logic and reason and sense… well, why shouldn't I enjoy it?

I don't need to give myself constant reminders of the past. After his confession last night, Stonehart seems ready to turn a new leaf. Who knows where that will bring us? All I know is that it will be infinitely better than anything we've had before.

There might be flare-ups in the future. There might be other instances of him getting angry or mad or vindictive. But I don't want to worry about that. I've already learned to savor these precious, short, exquisite moments with him.

He takes my hand. "Shall we go?"

I nod dumbly. I can't get my bearings with the man.

"Cat got your tongue?" he asks, a tiny bit of amusement clear in his voice.

"No," I say. "It's just you."

That comment makes Stonehart beam. "I have a gift for you," he says. "But I'm saving it for later tonight."

"You're spoiling me," I say as we come to the elevator. "A trip to Portland. Dinner in public. What's next, the collar coming off?"

Stonehart goes stiff. His eyes darken, and his whole demeanor changes.

*Idiot!* I think. *What possessed you to say something like that?*

"Jeremy, I'm sorry," I backtrack, as quickly as I can. "It was a joke. I didn't mean —"

"No." Stonehart cuts me off with one soft word

that's sharper than any knife. "You did mean it, Lilly, and I don't want you to lie to me again. I know what the collar means to you. And I also know — as you must — that it can never come off. I'm taking you out tonight to demonstrate some of that trust I spoke of. But this…" one finger runs around the collar, "must always remain in place. I did not become the man I am by not planning for contingencies. The collar ensures your compliance with my desires… no matter your disposition."

The elevator doors open and Stonehart steps through. He does not look at me when he continues. "You understand the need for it, I'm sure. You're a sharp girl. If you looked at things from my perspective, you wouldn't ask questions like that."

"I'm sorry," I say again. "It was just a joke. A bad one."

"Yes," he agrees. "A bad one." He takes a deep breath and hits the call button. The elevator starts to descend. "I do not want your attention diverted by such things, Lilly," he says. "Not tonight." He looks over at me, and then reaches out to take my hand again. "Tonight is supposed to be about us. A man and a woman enjoying each other's company. Nothing more. What can be simpler than that?

*What indeed?* I wonder. No matter how much I or Stonehart might want things to be different, our relationship can never be that black and white.

"Okay," I say instead, not giving voice to my doubts. "I can do that."

Stonehart smiles. There's something a little forced about that smile, I think when I see it, but I don't have time to dwell on it. The elevator doors open and I'm greeted by a long, black limousine waiting in the garage.

Stonehart places his hand on the small of my back and leads me out. As he opens the door for me, I catch a whiff of his cologne. It's different from before… very subtle, yet defined. A hint of maple and spruce. It's not a combination I would ever think went well together, but he makes it work.

At least, it works for me. It might be his pheromones underneath.

He settles down across from me and stretches out his long legs. The driver starts out into the city as soon as Stonehart shuts the door.

He looks at me. His gaze is electrifying.

"Do you feel that?" he asks.

I blink. "Feel what?"

"The energy… the thrumming… complete

between us. I've never experienced anything like it before. No other woman has ever affected me like that before." He leans forward, suddenly alert and intense. "Tell me it's not just me. Tell me you feel it too, Lilly-flower."

With his attention fastened on me, and him all but breathing me in, how can I deny it? He knows how I responded to his kiss.

A wave of heat overtakes my body as I have the sudden image of Stonehart pouncing on me, ripping off my dress, and fucking me right there in the back of the limo.

I blush, flustered, and look away. "I feel it," I admit shyly.

Stonehart shifts across the cabin floor and lowers himself next to me. My heartbeat ratchets up from his proximity. "What do you feel?" he presses.

There's a raw edge to his speech. "Describe it for me, Lilly." His hand comes to rest just above my knee. "Tell me how I make you feel."

My breaths are coming faster, now. They're deeper, too, making my breasts heave with every inhale.

"I feel... lost, "I say. Stonehart's hand tightens on my leg. "Lost in you. In your power. In your masculinity." Those are the words I'm certain he wants to hear, but it's not like I'm making them up on the spot. I'm not pretending. I'm telling him the truth. "You overwhelm me, Jeremy. You're larger than life. Your presence alone..." I swallow as his hand moves up my thigh, toward the spot where blood is now pooling, "...makes me feel exposed. Vulnerable. Only for you."

"Yes," he says, moving closer to me. I can feel his

breath on my cheek. His hand inches further and further under my dress. "What else?"

"I—"

I'm cut off as a blaring honk shakes the cab. The limo swerves, throwing me away from Stonehart and breaking the intensity of the moment.

"Fuck!" Stonehart curses. He turns around and pounds the window separating us from the chauffeur. "What the hell was that?"

The tinted glass slides down. An unsteady voice answers him. "Sorry boss. Some asshole decided to cut us off. It was a near miss."

"See that it doesn't happen again," Stonehart growls. The window rolls back up.

By now, I've already pushed myself upright. But my body feels strung out from the release of adrenaline. I feel shaky, and not in a good way.

Stonehart looks at me. He runs a hand through his hair. "That was... unfortunate," he finally says. "I'm sorry."

"You can't control traffic," I say. "You're not a god."

His lips form a thin line. "No," he agrees. "That I am not."

I feel a distance developing between us. I don't know whether to be thankful or disappointed.

He moves to his original seat across from me. His jaw is set as his eyes take me in.

"We have to go over the rules of tonight's engagement," he says.

"Oh." My voice is small. "I see."

"I hate taking you out of the moment — but it is

necessary."

"I understand." Secretly, I wish that his body were still beside me, with his hand crawling up my leg.

I straighten my shoulders to show him that I'm paying attention. "Tell me your rules for my behavior."

"They're simple," he says. "I find simplicity is best when dealing with complex situations. One. When you are at my side, you are not to speak to anyone other than me. If you are asked a question, you may respond with a single-word answer. Yes or no will do. I will handle anything more complicated. All you need to do is smile."

"Okay," I say. "That makes sense. I can do that."

"Two. I've taken measures to ensure that there are no…" he moves his tongue over his teeth, searching

135

for the right word, "...*temptations* for you, at the restaurant tonight. You understand that you must not reveal the details or your relationship with me to anyone. Furthermore, the ban on news of the outside world still stands. You will find no televisions or newspapers inside. Current events should be of no concern or interest to you. Do you understand?"

*I understand that calculating Stonehart is back,* I think. "Yes," I tell him.

"Third. I want you to enjoy yourself. I know this is a big step for us. Your behavior tonight will determine how we proceed when we return to California. You will be at the restaurant with me, but there will be other people around. It is the first time you will find yourself in such a position. If you even think of alerting anybody of your situation..." his eyes move down to my mouth, then down to the brooch, then back up to the collar, "...just remember

136

what I can still do to you."

I swallow and nod. The collar feels tighter than it has for weeks.

Stonehart relents. Just a tiny bit. "But honestly," he says, leaning back, "Just use your common sense. I want to be able to trust you, Lilly, not to act against me. It will take time for that trust to develop. We *will* get there, eventually. We'll take small steps, at first. And if you have doubts about what you should do, or how you should act... just ask. I'm going to be right there with you the entire time."

"I can do that," I confirm.

Stonehart is no fool. He knows the risk he's taking by bringing me out tonight. It's on me not to screw it up. If there's even a glimpse of a chance to run, or escape... I won't take it.

Because I know he will find me again. He will find

me, and he will be angry. He's been watching me for years. If I truly want to strike at him, I have to be patient. Running will grant me nothing.

But ingratiating myself in Stonehart's good graces? That will provide me the platform needed to destroy his entire world.

Stonehart chuckles. The sound brings my attention back to him.

"I recognize that look," he says. "What I wouldn't give to know what's going on inside your pretty little head right now."

"All you have to do is ask and I'll tell you the truth," I say quickly, trying to deflect attention away from my guilty thoughts.

"Yes, but not in its entirety. Isn't that so?" Stonehart reaches for the mini-fridge. "Champagne?"

***

Our hotel was pretty much in the heart of downtown Portland, so when the limo takes a turn away from the city, a feeling of apprehension comes over me.

"Didn't you say we'd be dining near the river?" I ask Stonehart. "I thought that was the other way."

"It is," he agrees. "I just planned a small detour first. I hope you don't mind."

"No," I mummer, but my thoughts start racing at breakneck speed. This trip was presented as an outing from the hotel to the restaurant. Nothing more.

What does Stonehart have planned? Why didn't

he tell me we weren't going straight to the restaurant?

I look at him. He's barely touched his drink, while mine is already half-empty.

I put the glass down. I am not going to allow myself to drink more than him. If I thought I needed lucidity before, just for the dinner, it's all the more important now that we're stopping somewhere else first.

"Can I ask where we're going?" I venture.

"You can." Stonehart smiles. "But I would be under no obligation to tell you."

The answer makes my hackles rise.

"I want it to be a surprise," he amends after a moment. "It's nothing unpleasant, Lilly. In fact, I think you'll find the experience quite enlightening."

*That* comment really sets the gears in motion. What would Stonehart consider 'enlightening'?

I guess I'll find out soon enough.

Ten minutes later, we're turning down a wide country road. Douglas firs line the sides. They are decorated with small, blinking Christmas lights. Only one other car passes us the entire way.

I see the lights from the complex first. They brighten the night from over the tops of the trees. We take one more turn, and the buildings become visible.

They are small and quaint. None of them stands taller than two stories. They have a Georgian finish that reminds me of the little bit of Harvard I saw when Fey and Sonja sneaked me to the football game. Around the perimeter of the community runs a solid brick wall.

The road we're on leads to wrought iron gates. They are closed. They start sliding open, specifically for us, when the limo gets close enough.

I look around for a sign or something that will give me a clue to what this place is, but find none. Even its name would be enough to give me some understanding of where we are.

I look across at Stonehart as we pass the manned guard booth. "Where are we?" I ask, my quaking voice betraying a hint of anxiety. "What is this place? A country club?"

Stonehart raises his eyebrows. "Not quite," he says. "But your guess is not far off, either."

"Well, it's some sort of private community," I say. I try to make my most pleading eyes at him. "Can't you tell me why we're here? You said yourself that trust is important to you."

"It is," he nods. "And right now, I need you to *trust* me when I say that we're here for good reason. As to the *why*... well, you don't want to ruin the surprise prematurely, do you?"

"After everything I've seen, I don't know how much I like surprises," I mutter.

Stonehart catches the comment. He smiles, then leans forward to take my hands in his.

"Lilly," he says, looking me deep in the eyes. "Truly, there is nothing for you to worry over. It's Christmas Day. Even the soldiers in World War I held off combat on the day of Christ's birth. Do you really believe I would ruin what we've begun to build by bringing you somewhere unpleasant?" The limo rolls to a stop before one of the brick buildings and the engine cuts off. "I have a friend here. I made a promise to him, long ago, that I would visit and chat at least once every year. Sadly, circumstance has prevented me from making good on that promise for the last few years. Tonight, in the spirit of Christmas, I hope to make it up to him. I take my word very seriously. If he were anybody else, I would have found some other way of keeping my promise, but... well, you'll see."

The driver opens the door and Stonehart steps out. He offers his arm to me, which I take.

"Don't forget your coat," Stonehart says, leaning back in the limo to retrieve the mass of furs that he insisted I take when we left the hotel. "I wouldn't want you to be uncomfortable."

My breath fogs in front of me in the chill night air. I hear the sounds of festivities inside — people talking, dishware clattering, music playing. It takes me an extra second to process the fact that I am now, for the first time in many, many months, within hearing distance of *other people*.

I'm afraid of becoming emotional. The fact that I am doing it with Stonehart's collar around my neck, and the man right beside me, makes it all the more surreal.

"Come on," he says, his footsteps crunching over the frost on the ground. "It's this way."

I let Stonehart guide me with a hand against my lower back. We walk toward the front of the building and climb the concrete steps to the grand double entrance doors. He stops just before reaching for the handle.

"I should warn you," he says, "not to be alarmed. Some of the occupants inside might seem a little…" his lips quirk in distaste, "…peculiar. I've tried to ensure that we won't be bothered by any such. But as

145

you so aptly noted yourself, I am not a god. I cannot control everything. Just know that I did my best."

Before I can reply, and ask what the hell he's talking about, Stonehart pushes open the door, and the sounds of a large gathering slam into me.

The walls of the building must be very thick, because inside, the clamor is deafening. Maybe part of it comes from the shock of seeing so many people gathered in one place.

The lobby clearly doubles as the common room. And Christmas celebrations are in full swing. There are lights draping all the walls. A massive tree stands in one corner, sparkling red and blue and white and complete with artificial snow. People young and old—though mostly old, I note—are moving around, chatting with friends, snacking on treats from the min-bar, reclining in circles of armchairs, bunching

146

up around coffee tables, laughing. There's a piano by one wall, and somebody is playing an upbeat version of "Winter Wonderland".

I see people in casual pants and cashmere sweaters, complete with the horribly-charming hand-knit designs and lurid colors that always accompany them.

It strikes me immediately that this is not the type of place I would ever expect to find Stonehart. These are not the people I would ever expect him to keep company with.

And, quickly shifting my eyes to him and back, I see that I'm right. The change in his expression is subtle, but I've become such an expert at picking up his intricacies that, to me, it's clear as day.

I see it in the added rigidness of his stance. In the tiny tightness around his eyes. In the way his lips purse, ever so slightly, as if he's just heard a tactless joke.

All that, I take in in the blink of an eye. What I find next alarms me more.

Not all is right in the festivities. I look at the exits leading away from the lobby and discover each one manned by a stationary guard. None is uniformed. But I can tell—from their standoffish demeanor, from the way their eyes glaze over the crowd, from the distracted way they interact with those nearby—that that is who they are.

Other things stand out, too. Small, subtle things, but they are enough to make the hairs on the back of my arms stand on end.

For example. The windows. The latches are outfitted with big, solid locks. Without a key, there's no way anybody would be able to open them from inside. They are not barred the way they might be in a prison, but the locks undoubtedly serve the same purpose.

What kind of place needs to have a lock-and-key mechanism on the windows from the *inside*?

I also see, cleverly hidden behind the various decorations on the walls, poster boards with thick lines of text. I can't make all the words out, but the font and spacing reminds me of the instruction boards found in pools: No Running Allowed, No Diving in The Shallow End, that sort of thing.

Last of all is the fact that our arrival has generated absolutely no notice whatsoever. None of the people so much as glanced our way when we walked through the doors. And, based on our clothes alone, we should definitely be worthy of attention.

"Here," Stonehart says, turning me to the side and

starting toward one of those manned exits. "Come this way, Lilly."

We stay to the outside of the throng of people. Not only do none of them look our way, but I notice two or three consciously lower their eyes when we come close.

The strangeness of it all definitely has me on edge.

Stonehart makes brief eye contact with the man I'd pegged as a security guard, and we walk past him with no comment or interaction. The hallway that we come upon is eerily abandoned.

As we get farther and farther away from the lobby, a haunting silence starts to replace the previous din. Stonehart doesn't speak. Soon, the only thing I can hear is the sound of my heels striking the linoleum floor.

We turn a corner to a second empty hall. This one,

however, has doors lining the sides. It reminds me of the hallways found in an apartment or hotel. There's a hint of staleness to the air. I shiver.

"What is this place?" I ask softly.

Stonehart's eyes flash at me. He does not answer, but that single look is enough for me to know that something is terribly, terribly wrong.

All of a sudden, the collar feels like it's attached to a countdown timer that will go off whether I abide by Jeremy's rules or not. Whether I stay within my boundaries or not.

"Jeremy?" I try, desperate to hear a single word out of him that might quell the panic building inside me. "Where are we?"

"In a place I've waited a long time to show you," he says. His voice is neither warm nor cold. But his eyes… his eyes terrify me.

151

They have the same glimmer of madness I saw when I met him at the restaurant for dinner so many months ago. The glimmer that hints at his cruelty, at his sadism, at a trap being laid. The glimmer that tells me he is in absolute control, and about to unleash some unknown horror my way.

"Right here, Lilly-flower," he says, stopping outside a door. My breaths are coming in quick succession. Sweat trickles down my back. And Stonehart's arm around my waist serves as the sturdiest shackle in the world. "We have finally arrived."

Stonehart steps forward, releasing me. He brings his wrist near the handle. A whirring sound fills the air, and the lock clicks open.

The last thing I see before Stonehart pushes open the door are the initials *P.H.* engraved on a tiny golden plaque right where the eyehole should be.

# Chapter Eight

On the other side is a small room. Stonehart guides me in with a bit of pressure on my back.

It's occupied. There is a man inside, sitting on the bed, facing away from us. Like everyone else so far, he does not look our way when we enter.

The door closes by itself behind us. The whirring sounds again, making me jump. We're locked in.

Only when the sounds fade does the man stir.

His head swivels toward us slowly. Lethargically. Like all the energy and life has been sapped out of him.

I notice his hair is speckled with grey. The skin on his neck is sallow. He is thin. Very, very thin.

His profile comes into view. The moment it does,

my knees give out. Stonehart's arm tightens around my waist, holding me up. He does not let me fall.

I barely notice. The man. I know that man. It's—

"Hello, Paul," Stonehart says.

I don't know what to think. I stare, aghast. Terrified.

Paul's eyes sweep over me without recognition. Of course not. Last time he saw me, I was an eleven-year-old girl. Aside from that forest rescue, he never paid much attention to what I did.

But I recognize him. Of course I do, after my first stint in the dark. That was when the suppressed memory—the real memory—of my fall came back.

I remember it clearly. It comes to me now. Paul's face, appearing in the gap above my head and blotting out the sun. That blasted crow. Paul, extending his arm, reaching for me beneath the earth. The words that come from his mouth:

*"Give me your hand, child!"*

Comparing the face I remember to the one I see before me now fills me with immeasurable dread. The underlying features are the same. He has the same wide jaw. The big, black eyes. The prominent forehead.

But the *vis vitae*, that critical life force that grants a person his personality… all of that has changed.

He has deep circles under his eyes. His cheeks are hollow. Gaunt. The skin beneath his eyes is slack, like he lost too much weight too fast. His complexion is ghostly white. He looks like he hasn't seen the sun in years.

The one thing I always remembered about Paul was that he was a big man. He had shoulders like a lumberjack, and a hearty laugh that could fill an entire room.

But this man… this version of Paul that I see before me… possesses none of those things. His eyes are empty and joyless. His girth is gone. He looks worse than a shell of the man I remember. He looks like a distant shadow. A specter. A wraith.

It's all too much for me. A wave of dizziness hits, and I sag against Stonehart like an ice cream cone left too long in the sun.

Paul's dim eyes focus on Stonehart. He blinks, as if in disbelief. And then his face lights up in pure joy.

He scrambles to his feet, suddenly full of energy, suddenly full of life. "Doctor Telfair," he exclaims. "It's you. It's really you!"

"Yes, Paul," Stonehart says gently. "It's really me."

"But… but how?" Paul stutters. "Why? I thought, after all these years, that you'd forgotten about me."

"No," Stonehart says. "I don't forget my friends, and I keep my promises. You must forgive me if my visits have been less frequent than I envisioned. I've been occupied."

"O-of course," Paul says. "I know you're a very important man. Why should you make time for little old me? But, truly…" he stops in front of Stonehart, staring at him with all kinds of adoration, "…it's an honor to see you again, sir."

"Please," Stonehart says. "You don't need to be so formal. We're all friends here, aren't we?"

"And you brought a companion," Paul says. His eyes dart to me. But, they never make it all the way to my face. He looks back at Stonehart before I can blink. "A beautiful woman, sir. I haven't had the pleasure of a lady's company in a very, very long time."

He reaches up and smooths his frazzled hair. "I'm... I'm afraid I don't know exactly how to act," he confides.

"Why Paul," Stonehart says, smiling wide, "you should relax. My guest and I came here to see you. Invite us to have a seat. Perhaps a cup of tea?"

"Oh, certainly, certainly," Paul mumbles, making an awkward bow. He licks his lips, clears his throat, and speaks in an oratory way. "Would you please sit with me? I've just put the kettle on. We will have hot tea in a minute."

He blinks, snapping out of the trance, and looks at Stonehart in the way an eager boy might at his father when he's searching for approval.

"How did I do?" he asks, his voice returning to

normal.

"Very well," Stonehart says. "I am pleased. And my guest and I will both graciously accept your kind offer."

Paul smiles and bows his head. He sweeps his hand low in an obsequious way, showing us our path.

By now, I've had enough time to recover. I take stock of the tiny room. There is the bed on which we found Paul. A small window is set in the opposite wall. It does not look like it can be opened. There's a single armchair, bolted to the floor. A small bookshelf, reaching only halfway to the ceiling, stands beside a reading lamp, which is also secured. There is a desk with a neat collection of notebooks on top, along with a wheeled office chair of dark leather.

That's it. There's nothing more. I spy some

expendable drawers peeking out from beneath the bed, which I take store some of Paul's belongings.

But the kettle? It's nowhere to be found. I don't even see an outlet other than the one for the lamp.

Paul directs us to his bed. I sit down with Stonehart in a daze, then watch, stunned, scared, and silent, as Paul starts preparing three invisible cups of invisible tea using an invisible tea kettle.

He brings the first cup to Stonehart, cradling it in his hands as if it were as precious as a newborn babe. Stonehart indulges the illusion, playing along so far to even bring the cup to his lips and pretend to take a sip.

"This is very good tea," he murmurs. Paul glances over his shoulder and smiles at the praise. Then, he carries the next cup to me.

My stomach is in knots. Time slows to a standstill

as he hands it over. He keeps his eyes down. "Careful now," he murmurs. "It's very hot."

I say something barely intelligible as I accept. Both my hands are shaking. My nerves are shot.

I know why things felt off in the common room. And I know, now, why Stonehart gave me the warning he did before we entered.

We are not simply in some gated community. We are in a mental institution.

What happened to Paul? How did he end up here? And, most important of all: what does he have to do with Stonehart?

I'm not ashamed to admit that, at this moment, I am more afraid than I have ever been in my life. Being trapped in the dark, even the first time, when I had no idea of the identity of my captor, does not compare.

It's a different, more menacing type of fear that consumes me now. The way Paul responds to Stonehart, the title he gives him, the way Stonehart sprang this on me, the way he lured me here with promises of a public dinner and all that bullshit about trust…

Obviously it means something. Just like my captivity means something. Stonehart and I have a shared past. But, it's one that only he knows.

That is what scares me most. I've now seen the extent to which Stonehart will go to to get what he wants. He chose me for a reason, and I'm certain that that reason is going to be revealed very soon.

The reason is not what I'm worried about. Stonehart's *intentions* are. I see Paul before me, a ghost from my past, downtrodden, subservient, mentally damaged, and it makes me wonder…

*Am I next?*

"Go on, Lilly." Stonehart's voice pulls me from my dark contemplations. "Take the tea. Paul brews one mean cup."

On hearing my name, Paul goes shock-still. I hear him draw a sharp intake of breath.

"Lilly…" he says, frozen in spot. "Did you just say… Lilly?"

My eyes dart from Paul to Stonehart. The man beside me has a look of utter triumph on his face.

"That's right, Paul," he confirms. His hand tightens on my knee. "I did. She is the guest I brought for you today."

"Not…" Paul's hands are at his sides. They're shaking harder than mine did when he handed me the imaginary tea cup. "Lilly… *Ryder?*"

*He remembers me,* I think.

"Yes," Stonehart says. "The one and the same."

I can feel him reveling in this moment.

"I promised you that you would see her when I left you here. Do you remember?"

"I—I do," Paul stutters. He turns to us. His eyes hover on me for a moment before going straight to Stonehart. "Of course I do. Remember? Hah!" he laughs. "I think about it every day. I think of *her* every single day. But I... I never expected such a gift. Such a magnificent gift. Th-thank you. Thank you, Doctor Telfair, sir!"

The excitement is palpable in Paul's entire demeanor. He's practically shaking with joy. But why? Why is he so happy to see me?

And if he is, how come he still hasn't met my eyes

once?

"I keep all my promises, Paul," Stonehart says calmly. "No matter the type of people I make them to."

Paul flinches at that. There is some sort of hidden dynamic between the two men that terrifies me. Being in this small room, with Paul, with Stonehart, terrifies me. But I am caught, just like a butterfly in a net.

Paul looks up at Stonehart again. Nervously, his eyes dart to me. My heart is beating so hard I'm afraid it'll rip free from my chest. Paul takes one step forward, cautious, in my direction. Then he adds one more.

"Nuh-uh," Stonehart says. He taps the side of his neck, just beneath his ear. "Careful now."

Paul stops immediately and turns a pasty white.

Even whiter than before. His eyes fill with terror as he looks at Stonehart. Unconsciously, his hands move to his own neck.

He swallows, and turns the turtleneck of his sweater down in one anxious motion.

That's when I see it. Beneath his sweater, I see…

A thin, black, seamless piece of plastic. Just like mine.

I gasp. My mind spins. I feel faint.

Paul has a collar, too. I am not the first person Stonehart has done this to.

If Stonehart notices my reaction, he gives no indication of it. He simply continues speaking, perfectly in control, as if this was the most normal encounter in the world.

"Did you know today is Christmas Day, Paul?"

Stonehart asks. "Have they told you that, in here? Do you keep track of time?"

"Christmas Day," Paul repeats, his words deathly hollow. "Yes. Yes, of course I do."

"It's customary to exchange gifts on such occasions," Stonehart says. "Do you have something prepared for me?"

"I—yes, yes. I do. I have just the thing." He turns back on us and hurries to his desk. He pulls open the top drawer and rummages through it, muttering to himself and shaking his head the entire time. He shuts it with a bang and attacks the one underneath.

The noises he's making intensify, getting louder, becoming angrier, until suddenly, with absolutely no warning, they cut off. He exhales a long, contented sigh of relief, and cradles something closely in his arms. Then he stands up straight and turns around.

"Now, don't laugh," he says. He looks only at Stonehart. His words are only for Stonehart. After the casual warning, it's like I don't exist to him anymore. "I made it especially for you. I had a feeling I'd be seeing you soon." He chuckles. "And my premonitions always come true."

Except, Paul isn't holding anything. His arms are empty. He approaches Stonehart, only a tiny bit wary, and hands him the imaginary gift.

"Hmm," Stonehart says. "Forgive me for asking, Paul, but I'm not quite sure what this is."

Paul looks absolutely scandalized. "It's a Christmas sweater," he says defensively. "Don't you see the patterns? I sewed them on the front just for you."

"Ah," Stonehart smiles. "I'm sorry. I must have had it inside out."

"Well. See that you don't when you put it on, you silly goose, you!" Paul giggles. The horrible feeling in my stomach is just continuing to grow. Paul is broken. He is utterly, completely broken.

"Try it on, please," Paul urges. "I want to see what it looks like on you."

"Very well." Stonehart stands. "Lilly, will you hold my jacket for me?" He begins to unbutton the front. "I would hate for my tuxedo to get wrinkled."

I glare at him, hatred filling every single cell of my body. Stonehart is responsible for Paul's condition. I am certain of it.

"No," I say, defiant and angry. "I refuse to be part of this charade any longer. Not until you tell me what's going on!"

Stonehart hisses a curse. Paul's eyes go wide. And then, the most incredible thing happens.

Paul collapses to the floor and starts to cry.

Stonehart grabs my elbow and yanks me up. His grip is tight enough to bruise. I try to squirm free, but he's so much stronger that I am. His eyes burn with fury.

He marches us to the door, stepping wide around Paul. He brings his wrist near the magnetic strip. The embedded entry scanner reads his biometric NFC chip and the mechanism works to open the door.

He thrusts it open and shoves me through. Before closing the door, he turns back to Paul and growls, "Compose yourself."

We're alone in the hallway when Stonehart turns to face me. He looks furious. Beyond livid. This is worse than I saw him when he found the dove.

He opens his mouth to speak — or likely, yell — then closes it again. He takes a breath. In through his nose, out through his mouth.

And that's all it takes for him to regain his composure. His eyes are still alight, but his words are icy cold.

"Did you not see," he says to me, "how *delicate* Paul's condition is?"

"Did you do it?" I erupt at him. I don't have his degree of self-control, or the years of experience honing my emotions. All I know is that mine are raging like wildfire. "Did you do that to him? Is he like that because of *you*?"

Stonehart at least has the decency to look shocked. Only for a brief moment, and barely enough for any but the most discerning observer to notice, but he does react to my accusation. Maybe there is a trace of humanity left under his masks, after all.

"No, Lilly," he scoffs. "Whatever power you

attribute to me, you let your imagination carry too far. I cannot do that to a man."

*Liar!* I want to scream. I just *know* Stonehart is responsible. It's a knowledge that comes from deep in my bones, from the very depths of my soul.

Instead, I turn the table on him. "Why did you bring me here?" I demand. "Why did Paul react that way when you told him my name? Why is he afraid to look at me?"

"Certain habits have been ingrained very thoroughly in our mutual friend," Stonehart explains levelly. "Respect and obedience are two of them. That is why he will not look at you without my express permission. As for his reaction? I was hoping he could tell you himself. Now, who knows how long it will take for him to recover."

Stonehart's eyes bore into me. He's challenging

me to a fight. I know he does not want me to be meek, not when it's so clear how riled up I am.

"So what?" I snap. "You didn't warn me. You gave no indication of how you wanted me to behave. For all your *planning,* Jeremy, it looks like this time things backfired on you."

A thin smile touches his lips. "Is that what you think? That I would let a little hurdle like this derail what I came here for? No, Lilly. We will achieve everything I intend with Paul tonight. Your little outburst in the room, however, will delay us. We might miss dinner."

"Oh, so that's still on the table?" I bark. "I have a hard time believing your greatest concern is missing a single meal. In fact, I don't even think you *had* a dinner planned. You just told me so to make me lower my guard, so that I would be caught completely unaware when you brought me here, instead." I glare at him. "That's the way of things, isn't it, Jeremy? I'm not blind or deaf. Nor am I stupid. I know how much these little mental games mean to you. You revel in the thrill of controlling, of manipulating others. Regular human interactions are a foreign concept to you. I know enough to know that you couldn't have built Stonehart Industries into the behemoth it is today were you just an ordinary man."

My heart is racing. Blood is pounding in my ears. My entire body is tight and tense with a mixture of adrenaline, anger, defiance, and... courage.

Courage is what allows me to speak my mind like this. Seeing Paul in there, seeing the miserable creature he has become has brought all my resolve back to the surface. I *will* challenge Stonehart. I *will* engage. I will make him see that, if he wanted a passive victim for his cruelty, he chose the wrong damn girl.

The only way I know to affect him is to make him see that, too. To reveal his actions, his own character to him, without a softening lens. To make him consider everything he's done from the perspective of somebody else.

"And you're not ordinary, Jeremy," I accuse, venom lacing every word. "You are a monster. A sociopath. It should be you in that fucking room—" One hand flies out to stab a finger at the doorway. "—not Paul."

Stonehart, for what it's worth, faces my tirade without a glimmer of emotion marring his face. His poker mask is back, and that makes him impossible to read.

I glare at him, waiting for him to say something.

Waiting for him to respond. Waiting to find out what my punishment will be for so clearly stepping out of line.

"So," he says after an endless, long, tense moment. "Finally, it seems you appreciate some of the finer qualities in me." One corner of his lips twitches up in a crooked smile. "I was wondering how much longer that would take."

My jaw drops. There is no explosion. No violent reaction. I just assaulted Stonehart with the most poisonous words that would come to me, and his response is to be... *amused*?

"What—"

He lifts a finger. Only one, but the simplicity of that motion speaks louder than words. I cut off.

"Don't press your luck," he warns. "I want you to take a silent minute to compose yourself. Then we can risk going back in there. And Lilly? Tread carefully. Wait until we're *outside* before speaking your mind again."

I narrow my eyes at him. What's he hinting at?

"I'm not going back," I say, crossing my arms. "I—"

"Two." Stonehart's voice is soft and slices through my protest like a frosted blade. He lifts a second finger. "I've been very generous with you, Lilly-flower. As proof of my new intentions. But if you think of testing my desires a third time tonight… the result will be very unpleasant. For us both. I don't want to backtrack with you again. I hate wasting my time."

He takes a large, menacing step toward me. I feel like I should run, but my feet are rooted to the spot.

Without warning, his hand juts out and grabs my

hair. He jerks me into him, puts his other hand on my ass, and kisses me.

I try to break away, but he has an iron grip. His kiss is harsh, uncompromising, and heated.

He lets go after only a few moments. I stagger away, unsteady from the assault.

"Gods," he breathes. "You know how I love seeing that spunk in you, Lilly. Nobody else, anywhere in my life, gives me that."

I huff and turn away, but I can't pretend that I'm completely unaffected. Even though I fought it, that short kiss did something to me, too.

I guess passion is greatest when emotions run high. I'm not going to forget that in the future.

After giving me time to adjust my hair, Stonehart steps to the door. "Ready?" he asks. "At my side,

Lilly. Now."

I avoid looking at him as I walk over.

"Good," he says, then leans in close to my ear. "Obedience is good when you know I need it. We're going to step inside once more. This time, watch what you say."

He swipes his wrist by the handle, the lock clicks open, and he leads me in.

Paul is… sitting on the bed, facing away from us, exactly the same way as when I first saw him. Nothing about the room gives any indication that a disturbance has occurred. The bed sheets are flat, smoothed over where Stonehart and I sat.

"Paul," Stonehart says. "You may rise and greet your guests."

Paul stands. There's a stiffness to the motion. He

turns around and stares at us. His eyes are empty once more.

"Paul," Stonehart coaxes. "It's good manners to say hello."

"Hello," he echoes, listless and hollow as ever.

"And to apologize for your previous behavior."

Paul's eyes go to the floor. "I'm sorry." He takes a deep breath. "I'm sorry you had to see that."

"It is forgiven!" Stonehart announces. At his words, Paul looks up again, anxious as a newly-trained pup.

"Will you invite us to take a seat?"

"Oh! Yes, yes. Please. Please, sit down." Paul steps away from the bed to give us room. "I'm afraid I wasn't expecting you again, Doctor Telfair. I did not set the kettle. We'll have to wait for the water to boil…"

He trails off and wrings his hands. "That's probably not good manners, either," he mutters, ashamed.

"You don't need to worry about that. Lilly and I won't be staying long."

"Lilly?" he repeats, sounding astounded. "Lilly's here?"

"Yes, Paul. She is."

"Can I… Can I see her?"

Stonehart gives a miniscule nod. "You may."

And for the first time, Paul shifts his gaze to me. He looks at me. Really at me.

"Lilly," he says. My name on his lips sounds almost like a prayer. He steps toward me, and brings a trembling hand to my cheek. There are tears in his eyes.

"My daughter."

# Chapter Nine

I reel back, breaking away from his touch.

"What?" I stammer. "What are you talking about? Jeremy, what's he talking abou…"

The remainder of my words die on my tongue as I get a look at Stonehart beside me. He's sitting straight, proud and triumphant in the moment. His eyes shine at me in their blackness, and the smug, knowing, satisfied smile that tugs on the corners of his lips tells me everything I need to know.

Paul is telling the truth.

All of a sudden, it becomes difficult to breathe. My chest tightens, and a horrible nauseous feeling builds in my stomach.

My vision blurs. The lights in the room become

vague, indistinctive points in a swelling darkness. My mind retreats, burrowing itself somewhere far away. Somewhere safe and distant and very, very far.

A lifeless gray starts to envelop me like a warm blanket. It offers escape. It offers safety.

But I can't retreat. Not now. I'm stronger than that. I have to be.

It takes all the willpower I possess to claw my way back to the surface. Tides and eddies of the strongest suppressed emotions threaten to pull me down. But I fight through them.

Eventually, my eyes regain their focus. I am back in the little claustrophobic chamber of a room.

Stonehart is speaking.

"...in accordance to our prior arrangement. I have

been told that you have been on your best behavior, Paul. Consider this, the fulfilment of my promise to you, as the final Token of Good Behavior you will receive."

Bile builds in my throat. *Stonehart gave Paul tokens, too?*

Paul nods eagerly. "Of course. Of course! I understand. I just did not expect to see Lilly… my precious Lilly…"

He starts tearing up again.

"How?" I whisper. "I mean you… you're really… my father?"

"Yes," he says through joyous tears. "Yes, Lilly. I am!"

The tightness in my chest threatens to make a comeback. "Where were you?" I choke out. "When I was growing up. When I was alone. Where were you?"

"I'm so sorry," Paul says. He sinks to his knees. "I'm sorry for everything, Lilly. For all that I've done. For all that I haven't given you."

Another change comes over Paul. Now, it's like *I* am the only one in the room for him. Stonehart might as well not exist.

*How did he get into such a fragile mental state?* I wonder in a daze. *What happened to him in the ten years since I saw him last?*

"You saved me once," I speak, nearly breathless. "That summer in the woods."

"You remember!" Paul gasps. "God bless you. You remember!"

"Why didn't you tell me…" my voice hitches

under stain of all the emotions I'm trying to keep in check, "…Why didn't you tell me who you were? You always ignored me! That entire summer at the cabin, you ignored me! Why did you always…" a sob comes out, "…always ignore me?"

"*Lilly.*" Stonehart's voice directs my attention to him. "Remember what I said. There is no need to yell. Paul will answer your questions so long as I allow it."

I give him a venomous glare. *As long as he allows it?* The man has been running my life from the shadows for God-knows-how-long. *Now* he has the nerve to interfere, in *this*?

"Go on, Paul," Stonehart says. "Your daughter deserves her answers."

"It was an agreement." Paul's eyes take on a faraway look as he steps into the past. "An agreement I made with your mother. I'm not a good man, Lilly. I have lived my life in sin. Temptations of the flesh always called to me. I was powerless against their allure. Their wonder."

He takes a deep breath. "When you were born, I had a… a substance problem. Your mother offered an ultimatum: our family, or the drugs. I made the wrong choice. I left you, my only daughter, my only Guiding Light in the world, the only thing I should have ever treasured, because I was weak. I did not know how much that choice would cost me.

"But your mother… she is a generous woman. Too generous, by far. She always had a big heart, Lilly.

"Years passed. And it was only a decade after you were born that I realized the mistake I had made. I crawled back to your mother on hands and knees, begging her to take me back, begging her to let me see you.

"And you know what she did? Do you know what that marvelous, amazing, beautiful woman did? She took pity on me. Like the great woman that she was. She took me in again, but only on one condition:

"That I would not reveal myself to you until I was one-hundred percent sober."

Moisture starts to well in the corner of my eyes. Paul's words are so heartfelt, so genuine, that there is absolutely no way that they can be the ramblings of a lunatic.

He really *is* my father. It's not a delusion like the tea kettle.

"So you see," he says, inching toward me and taking my hands in his. "You see, that was why things were the way they were. That was why I couldn't tell you earlier. And that summer? The summer we spent at the cabin? I was getting close then, Lilly. I'd been sober for six weeks. *Eight* was the milestone your mother set for me. If I could abstain for two full months, I could tell you who I was. We could be a family for the first time.

"But…" he takes a shuddery breath. "But having you go missing, all through the night, it terrified me. After I found you, I had a relapse. Your mother took you and left.

"You can't be mad at her, Lilly. You *mustn't* be. She only did it to protect you. Don't you see? She knew me better than I did myself. She knew I was not strong enough to resist the calling that had defined my entire life. She didn't want you to know, because she did not want you to suffer the ultimate disappointment when I let you down. When I showed my true nature."

He stops talking. I just stare at him, stunned. The fanciful story… it makes sense. My mother's behavior in the aftermath of her breakup with Paul makes sense. The lies she told me about him afterward make sense. The false memories she successfully planted in my head about him make sense.

They were her way of coping. She was the one who needed protection, not me. Paul, whatever his faults, was so much better than all the other boyfriends she'd had. More than that. He was the father of her daughter. Hope that things might be different was what let her take him back. And the crushing blow when the realization hit that he was ever the same man was what propelled her spiral into alcoholism.

How ironic it is that the one thing that kept Paul away was ultimately the same thing that destroyed her relationship with me.

"But now…" a tremulous smile comes over Paul's face. "Now, we've been reunited, my precious Lilly. Thanks to Doctor Telfair. It's been more than five years since my last drink. Did you know that? Doctor Telfair told me, he promised me, that if I could repent my sins, I would be able to see you. I've dreamed of nothing else since. And now, today…" the tears are flowing freely now, "Here you are."

He chokes down a sob. "I couldn't have done it without Doctor Telfair . I owe him everything." Paul glances at Stonehart. The look is full of unbridled admiration. "He is a great man. As great as your mother. He saved me. I owe my life to him. And now…" he brings my hands to his cheek, "…I owe my daughter to him, too."

*That's not all you owe* him. I think of the collar. Of Paul's collar. Of my own.

"I think that's enough," Stonehart interrupts. Paul flinches back. "Lilly, we have a dinner to attend. If we still intend to make the reservation, we cannot delay any longer."

He stands up. Paul scrambles away, almost in fear.

*My father,* I think vaguely. *What did Stonehart do to you?*

At that very instant, the strongest sense of purpose I have ever felt surges through me. I will discover Stonehart's true motives. I will make him cower before me. I will make him tremble. I will destroy everything and anything that he holds dear.

Not for me. Not for myself. Not even for vengeance.

But for Paul.

# Chapter Ten

Back in the limo, Stonehart appears very, very pleased with himself.

"You're awfully quiet," he comments.

"I'm thinking!" I snap.

Everything that's happened after leaving Paul has been a blur. I barely remember the walk out of the complex. I couldn't say if there were any interactions with the staff.

One thing stands out, though. We did not leave the way we came. This time, Stonehart led me through what was obviously the main reception room—the main entrance for guests and visitors to the place. I saw the name of the institution on the wall:

*Cedar Woods Academy.*

Beneath it was a list of all the major benefactors. It came as no surprise that Stonehart Industries topped the list.

The revelation that Paul is my father should have had a greater effect on me. But after everything I've faced, after everything I've seen, I think I've developed a sort of immunity to such surprises.

Besides, that's not what concerns me most. A huge — an enormous — piece of the puzzle has been revealed. But the overall mosaic is still shrouded in shadow.

It's obvious that Stonehart has a connection to me. To Paul. To my mother?

A tide of fear washes over me. Am I about the find out that she is a victim of the man's madness, too?

"My mother," I begin…

" —Has nothing to do with this," Stonehart says. His cruel eyes reflect the Christmas lights from outside and seem to shine red like a demon's. "Don't you see, my Lilly-flower, my Lilly dear? The only people who matter to me right now…" he spreads his hands, "…were contained in that very room."

His smile lingers for a long time. Then, he adds, "As for further reunions, well, you should not be expecting any more, any time soon."

"Paul called you something else. Doctor Telfair. Why?"

"Isn't it obvious? That is who he believes I am."

"Why, Jeremy? What does Paul have to do with this? With any of this?"

I hesitate for a flicker of a second, debating the

necessity of my next question. It's in direct violation of the rules he laid out at our first interaction.

I ask it anyway.

"What do *I* have to do with any of this?"

Stonehart laughs. "Now, now," he says. "You don't think I'd give away the mystery so easily, do you? Everything has a time and place, Lilly. When the pieces are in position… when the actors are ready and the stage is set… all shall be revealed."

"You want me to be frightened, don't you?" I whisper. I'm not speaking softly out of fear, but out of the firmest resolve. "It's all about power and control for you. It's all about the damned head games. You kept me in the dark because it gives you pleasure to see me uncertain." My voice is growing stronger and stronger with each sentence. "You did it to show how powerful you are, how strong, how cunning. Didn't you, Jeremy? But I know your weakness. I know what you really want. You crave attention. Everything you've done with your life has stemmed from that, hasn't it? You told me about your brothers and your father. You told me how he ignored you, how you were passed over time and time again. The story didn't hold meaning to me at first because I did not know you as I do now.

"But now it does. I've seen your true nature. Dominance and manipulation give you a thrill. But I know your secret. You *must* be witnessed. You *must* be a spectacle.

"At the same time, you're afraid. Afraid of losing control, afraid of not having that attention. That is why *this*—" I tug angrily at my collar, "—holds such meaning to you. That is why you say you want to trust me but make no mention of taking the collar off. Because it guarantees my compliance." I laugh, almost hysterically. "Of course it does. Of course! And how simple it must be for you. Push a button on your phone, and your poor slave girl will topple over in a seizure. Of course you'll get what you want from me then. You'll have your audience. Because, really…" I stare hard at him, "…who else can ever be allowed to see what you do to me, if not for the victim herself?"

Stonehart remains silent during my latest tirade. When I'm done, and breathing hard, he simply reaches into his pocket and takes out his phone.

My gut clenches up. The worst feeling of dread comes over me. Now I've done it. Now I've pushed too far. Any second now, the current will come on, and the most horrible pain imaginable will consume me…

"You think you understand me, Lilly?" Stonehart

asks. He raises his eyes to meet mine and speaks softly. "You think I want you to be frightened?

"No. That's where you're wrong. I don't want you to be frightened of me. I want you to be frightened of what I can *do*."

A noise from the right makes me jump halfway out of the seat. My heart is pounding hard when I look over. I find a small LCD television screen being lowered from its hidden compartment above me.

"It is a fine distinction, Lilly, but I'm going to demonstrate it to you. Watch."

The screen turns on. It's a video feed of Paul's room.

There's no sound. But I see Paul walking around in small circles, gesturing with his hands, his mouth moving as if he's in an intense debate with someone else.

"This is live, by the way," Stonehart says. "As you can see, Paul's mental state renders him unfit for regular interactions with most other residents. The doctors understand his hallucinations and schizophrenia. What they don't understand… are the convulsive fits."

Stonehart taps his phone. Immediately, Paul crashed to the floor. His limbs flail around wildly. His body convulses with the powerful current. He screams.

"No!" I cry out. "No! No! Stop it! No, Jeremy! Don't!"

"No?" He perks an eyebrow at me.

Then he taps his phone again.

Paul goes still. His chest heaves up and down in labored breath.

I stare at Stonehart, horrified. Adrenaline is rushing through my entire body after the display.

"Oh, you're going to love this next part," Stonehart says. He turns his attention back to the screen. "Right… about… now."

As if on cue, the doors to Paul's rooms burst open. Three uniformed staff members rush in. They move with practiced efficiency. Two grab Paul and lift him to the bed. He fights them, but he is no match. The third takes out a single-use injection pen and jabs it hard into Paul's thigh.

Paul's movements slow. His eyes droop shut, and he goes still.

The staff members wait a moment to make sure the sedative is in full effect, and then file out the room, leaving my father comatose and alone on the bed.

"The collar is a gift given to Cedar Woods from Stonehart Industries," Stonehart explains. His voice is smooth and gives absolutely no hint at any underlying emotions. "It's quite an ingenious device, really. An invention of Zigtech. Inside, it contains a tiny system of gyroscopes that continuously give it power. Movement of any sort recharges it. It never needs to come off. Which makes it very valuable to the staff at Cedar Woods.

"They believe that it informs them of Paul's current condition. When he's had one of his…" Stonehart stretches his neck from side to side, drawing out the sentence, "…unfortunate fits, a small alarm goes off to tell them they must come. The sedative is for his own good, you see. So that he does not hurt himself when he's upset. And he gets quite upset, naturally, following one of his fits. He starts rambling about secret watchers and electrical currents, but, you know." Stonehart shrugs. "Those are just symptoms of his mania."

"Monster," I breathe. "You're... inhuman."

"I am neither one, nor the other, Lilly. I am simply a man who knows what he wants." The screen turns off. "You mustn't worry much, though. Your father's condition has been dramatically improving. Why, this is the first fit he's had in nearly a year."

"You electrocute him for fun," I say. "Just like you do to me."

"No, Lilly." The words come out harsh and uncompromising. "That's where you're wrong. I take no pleasure in causing pain. But bad behavior must be eliminated, and this is the best way I know how."

"You're sick."

"And you were infatuated with me just a few

short hours ago." He examines his fingernails beneath a smile. "Tell me, which one of us is really twisted, here?"

The limo stops in an unremarkable alley in the heart of downtown. I hadn't even realized we were in the city already.

"Ah." Stonehart looks up. "It seems we've finally arrived. Remember what you just saw, Lilly, and know that your behavior with me now affects more than just you."

# Chapter Eleven

Dinner is a tense, strained affair. The excitement I had before over being out among people has been eliminated by everything that's happened earlier.

Stonehart was right when he said he took precautions to prevent temptations. The hostess greets us and quickly ushers us in along the far wall, away from the other occupants. We climb a set of stairs that were roped off, and emerge on the second floor.

This is clearly the more expensive part of the restaurant. The décor screams luxury. Low lights and soothing music provide a perfect atmosphere for secluded lovers.

Except, every single table on this floor is empty. I should have figured.

*Of course he bought out the second level tonight,* I think sourly.

We sit down at an elevated table close to a massive window. I can see the river below and the clear sky speckled with stars above. If I were in an even slightly better mood, I would be in awe of the natural beauty.

Stonehart speaks to the waiter. I don't listen. A glass of wine is set before me. With bitterness, I remember what happened the last time I accepted a drink at a restaurant with Jeremy Stonehart.

"So." Stonehart looks at me after the waiter leaves. "This has been a very productive trip for us so far. Wouldn't you say?"

I glare across the table. "I hate you," I declare.

He chuckles. "A reasonable claim. But false, I think."

"No," I challenge. "I really, really hate you."

Stonehart smirks and leans back. "You find me fascinating."

"Stop flattering yourself."

"I don't need to when you do it so well for me. You're curious, Lilly. Inquisitive. You want to know what makes me tick. Put that psychology education to use. Tell me what you see in me. Your analysis on the ride here was quite compelling."

"I don't have to do anything of the sort," I say.

"Oh, but you do, sweet Lilly. Did you forget the terms of our contract?"

And there it is again. *The Contract*. Of course it never disappeared. It was just buried somewhere in the background.

"Right now," Stonehart continues. "That is what I

ask of you."

"Fine. You want to know what I think? I think you're manipulative and sadistic. Everything you told me yesterday... the things you said after Rose and Charles left... those were all lies, weren't they? Lies meant to butter me up. So that I would lower my guard and be vulnerable for the surprise visit you had in store for me today.

"Because that was the true purpose of this trip, wasn't it, Jeremy? It wasn't to show me your 'trust'. It definitely wasn't to show repentance. It was to bring me to Portland... to show me Paul."

He tilts his head slightly to one side and fixes me with that dark, penetrating stare. I'm suddenly glad for the table separating us.

"You're right," he says quietly. "The visit to Cedar Woods did guide my intentions. But you cannot mistake my honesty with you yesterday. The things I said last night were true. I am a man of my word. I would not lie to you outright."

I scoff. "Somehow, I find that hard to believe."

"Then you know much less about me than you assume." Stonehart looks out over the water. "Really, Lilly, has this trip been so unbearable for you? I let you meet your father. I brought you with me to a public outing. We may have missed the gala last month. But, there will be opportunities to make up for that in the future.

"Yesterday, I allowed you out of the sunroom. Today, I have given you unprecedented leeway in speaking your mind. I have not been angered once, though many of your comments were clearly meant to incite me.

"No, Lilly," he continues. "I told you the truth

when I said I valued your spunk. And, against all my original intentions, you have become… *precious*… to me. You are a wonder the likes of which I have never experienced before."

"And you're an absolute madman," I counter. "How can you speak that way? How can you say those things after what I saw you do to my fa—"

I cut off. I don't want Stonehart to have any clue of my growing attachment toward Paul. That is a weakness he will have no qualms about exploiting, as he's already shown me.

"After what I saw you do to Paul," I correct.

"Again, you misplace blame. I am not the one responsible for what happened to you *father*." He emphasizes the word. "You are. As you will be every single time it happens in the future."

"You put him there," I say. "He wouldn't be in

that mental institution if it wasn't for you. And you expect me to be grateful? Hah!"

"He would, Lilly," Stonehart tells me. "Either that, or he would be dead. I am not the one who broke his mind. The drugs did that. Besides..." he picks up his wineglass and peers inside, "...you heard him yourself. I saved him. He owes his life to me."

"Lies!" I hiss, slamming one hand on the table.

Stonehart's gaze snaps to me. "No. They are not. I found him when he was in the darkest place imaginable. I helped him recover. Almost five years of sobriety, owed entirely to me."

"You slapped the collar around his neck!"

"A necessity," Stonehart says. "And a precaution. You saw how it became useful today."

"You're sick."

"I think we've already established that," Stonehart muses. "Don't you have any new adjectives for me? Here, I'll give you some to try: Demented. Abusive. Perverse. Cruel. All those fit your impression of me so far, don't they?"

"That and more," I spit.

He laughs. " 'That and more.' Well, I certainly can't expect you to choose any others before seeing a different side of me." He reaches into his inner-tuxedo pocket and takes out a sealed, white envelope. He slides it toward me.

I stare at it without moving. "What is that?"

"A proposal," Stonehart says. "Open it."

"No."

"Lilly." His lips come together to make a firm line. "Don't be childish. Open the envelope."

I glare at him but do as he says. I edge my knife under the flap, dismissing thoughts of using the cutlery as a weapon, and take out the two small slips of paper contained inside.

They're airline tickets. I look at them suspiciously, then back at Stonehart.

"Of course, we won't be travelling commercial," he says. "But I thought this would be a good way of showing you my intentions."

"What intentions?" I ask warily.

He sighs, as if suddenly tired. "Stop being obtuse. The act was charming at first, but now it's growing thin. You can be angry with me, I won't blame you. You are human, after all, and moreover, are prone to…" his mouth twists in a sneer, "…*womanly* emotions. I'd expect no less from somebody so young."

"Oh, so is that it, now?" I say. "I'm not mature enough for you? Is that why you want five years, Jeremy? So you can carve me into the woman you think I should be?" I laugh. "Or is it more sinister than that? What are your intentions, Jeremy Stonehart, truly? Oh, but I forgot — I'm not *allowed* to know. You just give me bits and pieces here and there and expect me to come up with some grand theory of why you chose me. Isn't that it? So that you can laugh at my naivety and bask in your obviously superior power.

"Unless you kill me first." My words are meant to wound. "Wouldn't that be convenient for you? Four and a half years from now, when I'm nearing the end of the *Contract*," I give special emphasis to that despicable word, "something happens to me on your grand estate. I'm sure it wouldn't be hard for you to make it look like an accident. Would it, Jeremy? Out there, in the privacy of your own home, it'd be all-too-easy to hide a body. It—"

"*Stop*." Stonehart's eyes are blazing. "You're hysterical. I am many things, Lilly, but a murderer is not one of them. If you ever bring this up again, I will punish you severely. You insult me. I won't be slighted based on your crazed fancies. I'm letting it slide, tonight, this one time, because you're clearly reeling from all the new freedoms I have given you. Maybe allowing you to speak your mind in the car was a mistake. I intended it as a demonstration of trust. Perhaps I misjudged your readiness. Do I need to establish rules for your conduct once more? That would be easy to do. One. You—"

"No. No, no, no." I shake my head quickly and lower my eyes. "You're right. I'm sorry. I shouldn't have said that. It won't happen again."

"Be thankful that I turned the brooch off before we left the hotel. If Rose, or anybody else, heard the way you conducted yourself with me tonight, I'd have no choice but to show you the consequences of making baseless accusations. Lilly. Look at me, Lilly! Meet my eyes!"

Slowly, hesitantly, I draw my gaze to him. Stonehart is directing his most intimidating glare at me. I suddenly feel very small, and very, very powerless.

What was I thinking, saying all those things? How could I have so carelessly given word to the dark thoughts that have been brewing in my mind for months?

"Do you understand?"

I should be thanking my lucky stars that he has taken all this so calmly. A man any less in control, who nonetheless exhibited Stonehart's sociopathic tendencies, would not be able to respond so... so *civilly*... to all that I've said.

"Yes." I nod. Then I swallow. "Thank you for your generosity."

He eases back. Slightly. "Now that that's settled," he says, "look at the tickets I got you."

I pick up the two airline passes and look them over.

*Departure: December 27, 2013. 0800H. Portland, Oregon (PDX).*

*Arrival: December 27, 2013. 1700H. Fort Lauderdale, Florida (FLL).*

"Florida?" I ask, puzzled. "You're taking me to

Florida?" I don't have the strength to consider the implications. By now, I know that I should just go with it.

"Yes." Stonehart smiles. "You didn't think I'd let Rose ruin the real surprise, did you? This is the trip I envisioned for us when considering your Christmas present. So there you go, Lilly. Merry Christmas."

\*\*\*

Dinner passes with no more unpleasantness. A tension exists between Stonehart and me. But, whereas I am negatively affected by it, he seems to thrive on it. It builds and culminates and comes to its natural climax back in the hotel room where Stonehart tears my clothes off and fucks me raw the moment we get in. His desire and passion is both powerful and overwhelming. He takes control of my body with no consideration for my state of mind.

Of course, I'd gotten used to that when I was in the dark. If there's one thing Stonehart taught me to do, it's detach all emotions and feelings from sex.

Much later, when he is slumbering beside me in the massive bed, I'm lying wide awake, staring at the ceiling, and trailing a finger back and forth over the smooth side of my collar.

Sleep is impossible. I keep thinking of Paul, of my mother, of my past. Trying to decipher how any of it can be connected to the virile man sharing my bed.

I sneak a glance at him, and then look away. Asleep, he looks almost human. Almost. Almost like any other man would. Nothing about his body or face gives any hint to the monstrosities he's responsible for.

It's astounding, really, that he trusts me enough not to do anything to him while he's so vulnerable. How easy it would be to sneak to the kitchen, find a sharp knife, and bring it back to the bedroom. I wouldn't even have to use it right away. I could hide it under my pillow, always within reach. Then, in the morning, when he inevitably wakes up hard and starts to put his hands on me…

I shake my head to change the trajectory of my thoughts. That would be easy, yes. Too easy. And where would it land me? My life would be forfeit. I'd be known as the harlot who murdered one of the most successful businessmen in the country. I'd go down in history with the Lee Harvey Oswalds of the world.

I am not that desperate. Not yet. I hope that I'll never be.

Seeing Paul renewed my sense of purpose. I don't want Stonehart dead. I want him damaged. I want him to suffer. I want him broken, irrevocably, mentally broken, the same way Paul is.

And I want to be the one responsible.

I lift the blanket off and step out of bed. I'm nude except for the collar. Stonehart says I'm not allowed to wear anything when I'm in his bed.

But there's a robe hanging off the closet door. I pick it up and go to the window, then look out over all the city lights. I have no idea what's going on in the world. Briefly, I consider Fey and Sonja. I wonder how they're holding up, what they're doing. If they tried to contact me for the holidays...

I sigh and turn away. Those aren't things I should be thinking about, either. The only thing that should concern me — the only thing that *does* concern me — is the person sharing the hotel suite with me tonight.

So, with that firmly in mind, I settle into an armchair and begin to plot.

# Chapter Twelve

If Stonehart is upset to find me out of bed the next morning, he gives no indication of it. I'm cheerful and full of energy as I pour him the coffee I'd brewed.

"I want to leave within the hour," he informs me. "I trust that'll give you enough time to get ready?"

"Yes, but all I have are clothes for this trip. Rose didn't pack me anything for warmer weather."

He gives me a look fit for a misbehaving child. "Do you really think I'd come unprepared? You'll find a full wardrobe waiting for you aboard the jet." He looks at his cups and quirks his lips. "You didn't spike this with something? Cyanide, perhaps?"

"Oh, Jeremy." I slap his arm playfully. "Don't be

so suspicious. It's perfectly safe."

He frowns at my uncharacteristic behavior, but makes no comment.

***

An hour later we're out of the hotel room. Three hours later we're in the air.

*Florida*, I think. *I wonder what's waiting for me in the sunshine state.*

Stonehart mostly ignores me during the flight, instead tending to business on his laptop and smartphone. With little in the way of mental stimulation available, and with me pretty much exhausted following my sleepless night, I close my eyes and try to nap.

The next thing I know, I'm being awakened by

Stonehart touching my arm. "Lilly," he says softly. "We've landed."

I struggle upright. "Already?"

"You were out the entire flight," he smiles. "I think our activities last night took their toll on you. I took the opportunity to wrap up some lingering issues at Stonehart Industries while you were asleep. For the next week, I am entirely yours.

"And you, sweet Lilly," he says, trailing a finger along my jawline, "are entirely mine."

His hand stops beneath my chin. He turns my head up.

Our eyes meet. He holds my gaze for a long moment. He seems to be searching my face for... something. What, I cannot tell.

"What did you get up to last night?" he muses to

himself. "After you left our bed?"

My chest seizes in sudden guilt. He can't suspect me yet. Can he?

But then I realize how stupid that worry is. Maybe I was too transparent when I greeted him this morning. But, there's no way he can read my thoughts.

He was right: I do tend to attribute too much power to him.

"Nothing," I say quickly, then blink and turn away.

"Hmm." Stonehart steps back and adjusts his jacket. "In either case, we're here. You should know that I've had this trip in mind from the moment I first saw you."

*When I didn't yet know you were watching?* I

wonder.

"Where are we going, Jeremy?" I ask. "What do you have ready for us in Florida?"

"Ah." He smiles again. "A bit of a red herring, that. Come now. It'll all make sense once we're outside."

I follow him off the jet. As soon as the doors open, I'm struck by the sudden humidity. And the heat. After the cool, air-conditioned interior of the cabin, the shift is quite jarring.

Of course, there's a limousine at the ready for us. This one is white. Stonehart walks me down the steps and opens the door, and then motions for me to go first. Our bags are loaded in the trunk by one of the flight attendants — Cindy, I think her name was.

Once that's done, we're off.

"The brooch looks lovely on you," Stonehart comments. "But we won't be needing it where we're going." He leans across and gently, almost tenderly, unclips it.

By now, the mystery is seriously getting to me. Didn't Stonehart say I have to have the brooch on at all times in public? And unless he brought me to Florida with intentions of never leaving his property—whatever it is—I don't see why I suddenly wouldn't need it.

Unless that *is* his intention. Maybe a week spent locked up together is his idea of romance.

Then again, *he* can come and go as he pleases. It's only I who have to be bound by the perimeter.

"Where are we going, Jeremy?" I ask again. "I think I deserve to know. Unless you plan on springing another *Paul*-esque surprise on me."

"No. My intentions are much less devious than that. In fact, you could say that they're quite simple. I merely want to spend an uninterrupted week with the woman who is quickly becoming the most important person in the world to me."

I scoff. "But all for your own hidden reasons, isn't that right?"

"My reasons are my own," he agrees. "I don't want concern with them spoiling our time together. For the next week, you are forbidden to make mention of them again."

I open my mouth to protest—then clamp it shut again. *It's just that easy for you, isn't it?* I think. *One word and the entire world jumps at your beck and call.*

*Well you just wait, Jeremy Stonehart. You wait. I'm going to strip you of your power. Somehow, some way, I will do it.*

*And then we'll see what type of man you really are.*

"Fine," I say. "But you still didn't answer me."

He chuckles. "Are you in a position to make such demands?"

"A clear answer for once would go a long way toward establishing that 'trust' you so frequently mention."

"Patience, my dear." He smiles and looks me up and down. "You must have patience. The ride won't take long. Look outside your window. Enjoy the view."

Grumbling to myself about Stonehart's incessant secrecy, I turn my attention outside. The limo has just left the private airfield and we're heading along a narrow road winding its way by the water. The ocean sparkles even in the dying light. I find myself thinking of the freedom it represents — a freedom permanently denied to me.

But freedom isn't what I crave any longer. Justice is. My own, personal blend of justice that will match Stonehart's depravity.

For that, I have to stay close to him.

We go along a wide bend in the road that curls along the coast. I see very few other vehicles. Anticipation about our final destination is killing me. Will it be another hotel? A condo on the beach? Some luxurious mansion Stonehart owns but rarely frequents?

Maybe it'll be a resort. A wild, crazy thought occurs to me: Could Stonehart have emptied an *entire resort* for the two of us?

I sneak a sidelong glance at him. I can't put it past the man. He certainly has the means to do it, and the motivation. It's the only way taking off the brooch would make sense.

*A billionaire,* I remind myself. *You're sharing a limo with a billionaire.*

More than a limo. I'm sharing my entire *life*.

It's funny — considering my upbringing — how infrequently I've thought of Stonehart that way. How many women would kill to be in my position? How many would eagerly sign their lives away on the dotted lines of *The Contract* just for the chance of even a minute of Jeremy Stonehart's attention?

*Too many,* I know for sure. *Like the secretary I found him fuckin –*

My thoughts come to a grinding halt. A wave of nausea and disgust washes over me. One thing we've never discussed in earnest was what I found going on in his office that night.

*Share a limo. Share a bed, share my life. Share a venereal disease.*

"Are you clean?" I burst out, without thinking.

Stonehart blinks. "Excuse me?"

"You gave me your bloodwork once before," I say. I think of the countless times he's fucked me without a condom. Which has been every single time. How many other women has he had on the side since then? "That was a very long time ago. Are you still clean?"

His mouth forms a thin line. "This is about Angelica, isn't it?"

"Just answer me, dammit!"

"No." The word comes as a savage growl. "Not before you tell me why now, of all times, you bring this up."

"Because I want to *know*, Jeremy!" I exclaim, exasperated.

"You should *know* that I want to keep you in perfect health."

"That's not what I asked you!" His deflections are so frustrating I could scream. "Just give me a straight answer. For once. Please. I have to know. For my own peace of mind."

"And if I'm not *clean*?" he challenges. "If I'm not, what difference would that make? None!" There's heat and ferocity in his voice of a kind I've never witnessed before. "You'd still be mine, Lilly. Your body would still belong to me. *You* would belong to me, for the length of the contract, for the subjugation of your debt. Don't you forget that. Don't you ever forget that."

"How can I forget?" I spit at him. I tug on the

collar around my neck. "This thing's still here, isn't it? And it will remain for however long you decide. It's a constant reminder that I'm not your lover. I'm not your woman. I'm your prisoner."

"A prisoner by your own hand," he snarls. "You signed the contract, Lilly, not I. I gave you a choice. I gave you an out."

"Starvation?" I laugh. "Dying in the dark? Is that what you call an 'out', Jeremy?"

"You're jealous." His eyes are storming. They pierce into me like jets of flame. "That's what this is about, isn't it? Jealousy. God! I thought we were past this, Lilly!"

"Jealous?" I scoff. "Of who? You and your *whores*?"

"THERE HAS ONLY BEEN ONE!" he screams.

The silence that comes next is deafening.

Jeremy's exclamation came like a thunderclap. It filled the insides of the cabin and shattered the tremulous tendrils of peace.

It's the first time I've heard Stonehart raise his voice like that. It's the first time I've seen him lose control.

He seems just as surprised as I am. He's breathing hard, clearly amped up. His hair is disarrayed. His nostrils flare with every exhale.

I suddenly feel very small, very vulnerable, and very, very alone.

I start to cry.

I don't know what brings it out of me. I've never been overly emotional before — at least, not outwardly so.

"Shit," Stonehart says softly. "Shit, Lilly, I'm sorry."

He starts to move along the seat toward me. "I—"

"Don't," I say. I dab at my eyes. "Don't apologize. I'm fine. I'm okay. Just… don't come any closer, okay? Not now."

Stonehart ignores my request. He shifts across to my side. His movements, however, are not predatory. And his eyes are soft.

I look away. I hate for him to see me like this. I'd hate for anyone to see me like this.

Sniffling, I try to stop the stupid little hiccups that make me sound so pathetic. I blink rapidly, trying to erase the tears.

All of a sudden I feel Stonehart's arm come around me. He pulls me toward him, but does not force it. I resist, at first, but… little by little… he coaxes me closer.

Without really knowing how I got there, I find myself pressed up against his body. It's hard and firm and — as much as I hate to admit it — comforting.

He lets me cry into him. He does not say a word.

He starts to stroke my hair. I feel his nose and mouth touch down atop my head.

"This is my fault," he whispers. "I don't enjoy seeing you like this. I'm sorry."

"It's just me," I blubber. "I'm being stupid." I start to push away. "I'll get over it. Just give me a second."

But he refuses to let me go. Instead, he tugs me even closer to him.

The solidity of his body serves, against all reason, as an anxiolytic. I guess some things and some reactions — the nature of being held to be comforted — are so deeply ingrained in us that in certain moments, our bodies are unable to distinguish who it really is doing the comforting.

Stonehart's deeply male scent fills my airways. I find that comforting, as well. I cry a little more, and then the ebb stops. In place of the tears comes a peculiar kind of peace.

"I shouldn't have yelled," Stonehart murmurs. His free hand finds mind and he grips it tight. "My father used to yell at my mother, did you know? He did it all the time, even more so after she became deaf. I always blamed him for that. And I promised myself that I would never degrade into the type of man who has to yell at a woman to be heard.

"So I'm sorry, Lilly. Truly, I am. I wouldn't regularly admit it, but your accusation… hurt."

"What accusation?" I ask softly.

"That I am having sex with other women behind your back." He grips my hand tighter. "It only happened once, and it was a mistake. I told you why I did it, but those reasons do not excuse the fault. It was wrong. And I am clean. I value my health very highly. An optimized body is key to a powerful mind."

"Why couldn't you just say that at the start?"

"Because." He makes a sound halfway between a grunt and a chuckle. "Because you should know better. Because, it was a stupid fucking question."

"Yeah," I say, pressing my face into his body. I laugh a tiny bit. "Yeah, I guess it was."

"You know how I detest sloppiness, my Lilly-flower," he says. "And you know how precious you are to me. I wouldn't do anything to put your health in harm's way. Not like that."

*Just in all the other myriad of ways you've invented,* a tiny, annoying voice squeaks in the back of my mind.

I shut it up.

The limo comes to a stop. I'd been so preoccupied that I hadn't even noticed that we had left the main road.

"We're here," Stonehart says.

I push off him and look out the window. "We're in a... marina?"

"Come on," he says. He twines his fingers through mine and helps me up. "Come on, let's forget about all this. I've planned quite a surprise for you, Lilly. I think—I hope—that you're going to love it."

We step outside. The sun is close to the horizon,

casting the final minutes of the day in a glorious, magnificent red.

Stonehart looks around, orienting himself, and then smiles and points. "There," he says.

I follow the direction of his finger. He's pointing at the very end of the pier, where the largest, most ostentatious yacht I've ever seen is floating in the water.

It must be forty, fifty feet in length, at least. It's moored away from all the other boats due to its sheer size. The dying sun reflects off its glossy, pristine hull, all in white.

Stonehart links arms with me and leads me forward. It only takes a few steps before the sun is hidden beyond the massive yacht, making it seem to glow like an incandescent pearl.

"That's yours?" I ask. Of course, I know by now to

expect only the grandest expressions of wealth from Stonehart.

"For the next week, it's *ours*," he corrects.

We climb aboard. The limousine driver ferries our luggage after us. I've never been on a boat before, much less a yacht, much less one as spectacular as this. Everything is shiny and new. The gold metal of the railing feels cool under my hand.

Stonehart shows me inside. It's all lacquered wood and whiter leather. The overhead lights, embedded in the ceiling, come on as soon as we enter.

"So?" he asks. "You're quiet. What do you think?"

"I've never been a fan of the open water," I hedge. Stonehart's eyes narrow. "But," I continue, breaking out in a smile, "I think this yacht might be enough to make me change my mind."

Stonehart laughs. "Come," he says. "I want to show you the bedroom. I have a feeling we'll be spending plenty of time in there."

***

I sleep late the next morning, and wake up alone.

Stonehart wined and dined me last night. The entire time, he was a perfect gentleman. There were no surprises, no unpleasantness. In fact, I can legitimately say that I enjoyed the hours I spent with him last night.

It felt a little like a continuation of the time we had together before his two-week trip. Before my massive blunder. Before the ensuing punishment.

Of course, things can never go back to that. I was

naïve back then. I was breaking, though not in the way that was clear to me. It was more subtle, more insidious than that. I was starting to believe, deep down, that maybe Stonehart could change. That maybe his behavior in the past could be forgiven.

I was seduced by the illusion of the man. By the illusion of the life he granted me. A giant mansion, a limitless estate, unlimited wealth… and him. At the heart of it, always him.

But he is not capable of change. A man who built himself up from nothing, who discarded his name before overthrowing his father, to whom vengeance and revenge mean so much…

No, I cannot expect Stonehart to change. Not in the way I thought he might, before.

But that doesn't matter now. I don't need him to change. I need him to remain exactly the same. I need to lure him into a false sense of security. And then, at the point he's most vulnerable… I will strike.

I yawn and stretch. Having sentiments like that doesn't mean I can't be comfortable in the present moment. It doesn't even mean that I can't enjoy moments, like last night, with Stonehart. Yet, seeing Paul… coupled with the revelation that he's my father… that will anchor me against Stonehart forever.

There's the collar, too. But as long as I watch my behavior, it's not going to hurt me.

One final thought occurs to me just as I'm about to get up: Paul might not even *be* my real father.

His story was certainly convincing. But his sanity is questionable. I saw the episode with the tea set. Who's to tell if the elaborate tale wasn't something that Stonehart implanted in his head to fuck with me?

But that's not the important bit. It doesn't matter if Paul is truly my father of not. He's a human being who once played a part in my life. And he is being manipulated, just as I am, by Stonehart.

That's what I will always remember. Seeing Paul thrashing on the floor was worse than when Stonehart showed me tapes of my own few days of captivity. Because it happened to someone else. Because I felt responsible for Stonehart's actions.

He doesn't know what the trip to Cedar Woods did to me. It changed things, irrevocably, between us. Whereas before, a tiny, nonsensical, and very emotional part of me might have held out hope that there really could be some sort of acceptable future between myself and Stonehart… one based on a relationship not defined by the contract… that part has been obliterated.

All for the better, for me. And for the worse, for Stonehart. I don't know what his intentions are or how they might have changed since I first arrived in his home. All I know is that I am more steadfast and resolute than I've ever been in my life. Thanks to Cedar Woods.

The only thing that comes close to the sense of purpose I feel now was in high school, when the drive to succeed, to not end up like my mother, propelled me to bury myself in my books and aim for the Ivy League. I made it. The acceptance letter from Yale was the final vindication of all my effort.

That was the greatest achievement of my life. The joy I felt, the satisfaction, it made all the sleepless nights and weekend study sessions spent as a hermit worthwhile.

I know it will be nothing compared to the feeling I get when I bring Stonehart down.

Applying to college was following a defined path. It was identifying a process and exploiting it, like so many others have done before.

There is no process for what I intend to do now. That makes it more exciting. I'm breaking new ground. I'm going head-to-head with a madman... who also happens to be one of the most successful business minds in the country.

It'll be my wits against his. My cunning against his cunning. My intellect against Stonehart's intellect.

It'll be a chance for me to prove, to myself, the type of woman I really am. I thought, some six, seven, eight-odd months ago, that my work with Corfu Consulting was my chance to showcase my abilities to the world.

But that was peanuts compared to this. The stakes are so much higher now. I've played the role of prisoner for long enough. Stonehart might think me tamed. Has he lowered his guard yet, as well?

Perhaps. Though, perhaps not. I cannot underestimate him. But what else would have prompted him to take me out of the mansion, to bring me to Portland, then to Florida, and then here?

I refuse to believe that his actions are as clear-cut as he claims. All that bullshit he spewed the night of the Christmas dinner… his nonsensical justification of his actions, the apology he gave me, the 'reason' for starting to be enamored with me… I know that's all a lie.

He showed who he truly is when he introduced me to Paul. He showed me that he can never change. He showed me that I was a fool for believing otherwise.

I smile, and get out of bed. I should thank him for that visit. Because, against his best intentions, and despite my near-hysterical reaction afterward… it was a watershed moment. It will stand out in my mind, as clear and hard as any diamond: The point when everything changed.

# Chapter Thirteen

After I shower and get dressed, I wander out to the deck of the yacht.

We're sailing over the water. A sense of alarm rifles through me when I realize that I can't see any land anywhere.

I hurry to the captain's quarters, where I discover Stonehart steering. He has a great big grin on his face. He's wearing white cargo shorts, boat shoes, and a baby-blue, casual t-shirt that's unbuttoned halfway exposing his chest. I catch a glimpse of his hard body through the V. Memories of last night's lovemaking come to me unbidden.

"Hello, beautiful." His smile widens when he sees me. "Enjoy your rest? It's a glorious morning."

He's right about that. The sun is bright. There's not a cloud in the sky. The air smells fresh and clean.

"Where are we going?" I ask.

"What, you couldn't think we'd stay moored to that dock forever? What's the point of a yacht if not to explore the open ocean? We're taking advantage of her power."

I frown at him, not from any great displeasure, but to show him that his shtick of avoiding answering my questions is growing old.

"You'll see soon enough," he tells me, kissing my crown. "For now, why don't you go lounge on the deck? The weather's perfect for sunbathing, and I would love to see that flawless body of yours in a tight little bikini."

***

'Soon enough' turns out to be four days later.

When the yacht continued sailing, all through that first day, I began to suspect that Florida was never our intended destination. But Stonehart deflected all questions about where we were going no matter how hard I tried to wring out an answer.

Aside from that small irritation, though, the days were generally agreeable. I showed no bitterness toward Stonehart, and he seemed to appreciate that. He would never say it out loud, but I began to suspect that, for all his posturing, he was as glad as I to inject a semblance of normalcy into our time together.

The surprise came some days later.

It was just after lunch when I first spotted the tiny islands dotting the horizon. They looked like pebbles from far away, As we approached, I began to make out their lush, green splendor. They were uninhabited. White sand covered the coasts and beaches, framed by enormous palms.

I ran to Stonehart the moment I saw them. He wouldn't say a word, but I knew from the twinkle in his eye that my reaction was exactly what he'd been hoping for.

As he expertly navigated the yacht through the waters, the hot sun shining brightly down on us, a palpable excitement started to form in the pit of my stomach. Growing up on the East Coast, where it was always cold save for the few precious months of summer, I had dreams of a tropical paradise. It was something my mother and I shared. Before our relationship collapsed, we would spend whole nights talking about scraping enough money together to buy a pair of tickets to the Caribbean, or the Cayman Islands, or somewhere warm where we could leave behind all the troubles of our day-to-day lives, just for a week or two.

It was never more than a pipe dream.

A wave of sadness washes over me with that thought. One of our biggest disagreements came when I was fifteen, a few years after she began drinking. That was about the time I started getting serious about my aspirations to build a better life for myself. Money, of course, was always a hot-button topic in our small, two-person family. The year before, I'd been working part time anywhere that would accept me, doing my best to help with rent. But that summer, before school began, I knew I had to make a choice. I could either keep working, and risk becoming my mother… or, I could start focusing solely on school, forget the odd jobs, and do everything I could to make a proper, educated woman out of myself.

We were barely scraping by as it was. So, when I announced my intentions to my mother, she became hysterical. I tried to ease her into it. But, there was no sugar-coating the truth. School had to come first. I could not keep working.

The blow came when, in a moment of severe indiscretion, I declared that maybe we'd have enough money for rent if she just had the self-control to lay off the booze.

I cringe at the memory of her reaction. If I thought she was hysterical before… well, it couldn't hold a candle to her reaction then. She went berserk. She told me to get out, that I was ungrateful, that I was a leech, a mooch, that I was no better than my deadbeat, good-for-nothing father.

It was the first time she'd ever made reference to him.

Obviously, even the strongest, most self-reliant fifteen-year-old would be crushed by such accusations — especially when they came from someone so close. I left the house in tears and spent the night with a friend. The next morning, when I slipped in quietly to pack my things, I found my mother waiting for me on my bed.

Her eyes were red. She looked like she'd been crying, too. She apologized the moment she saw me, told me that she didn't mean what she'd said, and begged me to forgive her. I did… But things were never the same again between us after the fight.

That's why the sudden appearance of the islands has such a strong effect on me. Coming to a place like this was a dream my mother and I shared, even if we both knew it was impossible. And now… being here, on this yacht, with Stonehart… it just… it just… gets to me.

"Lilly. Lilly, are you all right? Lilly!"

I shake my head and snap to attention. Somehow, I've ended up on the floor. Stonehart is kneeling beside me, his hands on my arms. Why am I on the floor?

"You wavered and fell," Stonehart says, as if reading my thoughts. Concern is plain on his face. "Must be the damned sun. You're overheated and dehydrated."

"No…" I shake my head. "No, it's nothing like that."

"Then what?" Stonehart poses.

"I... don't know. I'm okay, though." I start to stand. Stonehart helps me. He doesn't let go even when I'm upright.

"You're not sick? How are you feeling? Here, let's get you in some shade..."

I let Stonehart lead me to a nearby beach chair shielded by an umbrella. He sets me down carefully, as if I'm a fragile, porcelain doll.

"Would you like some water?"

I give a small nod.

"Stay right here. Don't move. I'll be right back."

I watch him hurry out of sight. He returns a moment later carrying a tall glass full of ice. He pours water from the nearby pitcher into it and hands it to me.

I cradle it with both hands. "Drink," Stonehart

says. There's undeniable command in his voice. I place my lips around the long metal straw and take a delicate sip.

He watches me intently. It strikes me at that moment, that right now, Stonehart is taking care of me. Stonehart. Taking *care* of me.

It's almost too much to believe.

"You need to be more careful," he scolds. But his words are soft. As he runs his hand over my smooth thigh, I feel a tingle of pleasure from his touch. "I would hate for anything to happen to you from an oversight on my part. From now on, we're going to limit your sun exposure."

"What, here?" I say, casting a look around at the pristine, sparkling waters surrounding us. "Good luck."

He chuckles. "In that case, we'll make sure you

have enough fluids in you. I need you strong and healthy, my dear Lilly-flower. I wouldn't know what to do with myself if you wilt."

I smile. That was sweet. "You know, despite evidence to the contrary, I'm not nearly so delicate as you might think."

"I know you're not," he says. "But I also know you're damned stubborn. You demonstrated that when you held out against the contract for as long as you did."

Involuntarily, I shy back. That was in the *past*, and though I'm never likely to forget it, hearing him refer to it is discomforting.

Stonehart catches my withdrawal. He curses under his breath. "Dammit woman, I'm not going to apologize for what I did to get you here. But haven't the last few days proven that things are different?"

*Maybe in your mind,* I think. The only answer I give him is a little nod.

He gets up. "Would you like to know our destination?"

"You mean, you're finally ready to tell me?"

"Not tell you," Stonehart says. He extends his hand to me. "Show you. Come here."

I take his hand and he pulls me up. As we walk toward the front of the yacht, he runs his thumb over my knuckles in a strangely endearing, yet oh-so-innocent fashion.

In the distance, but so much closer now than I remember stands a beautiful, uninhabited island. At least, that's what I think at first. It takes me an extra second to pick out the little hut that's cradled in a nook of the shore.

Then I realize how far away we still are, and it dawns on me that the hut is not so little. Stonehart has turned the engine off. But, we're still floating onward, propelled by both our momentum and the tide.

"That," Stonehart says, his eyes shining, "is our destination."

"It's yours?" I ask. I know it's a stupid question, but it gives me something to say.

Stonehart gestures around us. "I own all of these islands," he says. Then, he hedges the proclamation a bit. "Rather, Stonehart Industries does. They were purchased by my real estate team at the dip of the 2008 recession. They made plans to build resorts on these shores and transform them into a magnificent tourist destination. Unfortunately, trouble with the locals got in the way."

"What happened?"

"The usual. They protested against us ruining nature's gift with commercialization. It was expected. I was ready to ignore them, until one day I had my pilot fly me over the land. I hadn't seen it before. I was immediately struck by its beauty. The protests made sense. I decided, instead, to keep all of these islands as a preservation. But for more selfish reasons than they ever knew.

"You see." He turns to me. "The moment I lay eyes on these islands, I knew that they were something special. They were purchased as a business investment, but during that flight I became enamored with them. And I had this image… this vision… of finding one woman to share them with."

He steps close to me. My heart starts pounding hard. "That woman, Lilly," he says, tilting my chin up, "is you."

And he sweeps down to kiss me. It's a kiss full of passion. Full of life. I cling onto his shoulders, drawing him close, intoxicated by the beauty of the moment and the sweetness of his words. Even if they are a lie. Even if they do come from a sinister place.

They still affect me.

Kind of how *he* affects me.

# Chapter Fourteen

The yacht lays anchor and we take a small raft to shore.

There's a small group of waving natives on the beach. Where they came from, I have no idea.

As we get closer, I see that it's one big family. There's a father, a mother, and four small kids: three boys and one girl.

"Who are they?" I ask Stonehart.

"Our housekeepers," he answers.

The kids race to the dock when we're close. They're laughing and yelling and genuinely excited about our arrival.

Stonehart picks the girl up and spins her around, then kneels down and speaks to her brothers.

"Encantado de conicerte"

My eyebrows go up. "¿Hablas español?"

"Enough to say hello," Stonehart winks. By now, the parents have reached us as well. The mother envelopes Stonehart in a hug and pulls him down to kiss his cheeks. The father shakes Stonehart's hand with both of his, bowing his head again and again and again and saying things I don't understand but that sound very flattering.

I stand back and watch, fascinated by the interaction. This feels more like a great family reunion than a land owner arriving at his estate.

While that's going on, the children shift their attention to me. Two of the boys are shy, hiding behind their mother's legs, while the little girl continues to be enamored by Stonehart. The third boy, however, who looks to be the oldest — though he can't be more than six or seven—comes up to me and tugs my hand.

I look down, startled to feel the little palm wrapped around my forefinger. He has something hidden behind his back.

I kneel down and smile. "Hello," I say. "What's your name?"

He giggles, looks at me, then back down at the sand, and then he sticks out his other hand.

In it is a beautiful, perfect shell. "For me?" I ask. He presses it into my palm. When I'm holding it, he blushes brightly and spins back to run to his brothers.

They start laughing as soon as he joins them, their voices loud and excited.

"Lilly." Stonehart is beside me again. I look up

and find that he's brought both mother and father with him.

"This is Manuela," he says. Then he switches dialects. "Manuela, conocer Lilly."

The woman—who barely reaches up to my chin—clasps my hand and shakes it tight. Then, without warning, she yanks me down and kisses both my cheeks. All the while, she's beaming and repeating the word, "Biutiful! Biutiful!" over and over again.

"And her husband Jose." Stonehart gestures to the man, who also smiles widely and shakes my hand more formally.

Introductions completed, we're distracted by the kids running back to join us. Two of them grab Stonehart's hand, and mine. They pull us toward the house in a flurry of excitement. Meanwhile, their father picks our bags up from the boat and carries them after us.

Manuela starts jabbering right away. I can't even distinguish the individual words she's saying, but Stonehart seems to have no trouble following along. He translates bits for me.

"Manuela says you're very beautiful. A pearl from the deepest waters. More stunning than any woman she's ever envisioned for me." He smirks. "I don't know why her expectations would be any lower."

We make our way toward the villa. I follow Stonehart in a kind of stunned daze. These people — this family — all worship him.

I see the way he interacts with the kids. The boys and little girl run circles around him. Not only does he not mind, but I think he actually *enjoys* the attention.

I've never seen anything like it. Never *expected* to

see anything like it. Not out of Stonehart.

But here on the island, he is a different man. Maybe the tropics are having their effect on him. Maybe it's the safety afforded by a place so remote. He doesn't have to be on guard. He has no image, no persona, to maintain.

As I reflect, I realize that, despite everything he's shown and done, it must be hard to *be* Stonehart. He's responsible for the day-to-day operations of one of the world's most prosperous and secretive companies. He built it from the ground up. He can't afford to show weakness, not in his professional life, nor in his personal life.

Especially since his personal life revolves around me.

But I can't allow myself to feel sympathy for him. He chose his own poison. But still, seeing him like this… it adds an unexpected touch of humanity to him.

A warm feeling starts to rise in my heart. I want to force it down, but the surrounding laughter, the pristine, palm-lined coast, the beautiful villa in front of us… won't let me. I can't help but feel, well, *happy*.

"They think you're a hero," I say to Stonehart when we're finally alone inside. The air conditioning provides a welcome relief from the heat.

Stonehart smiles. He sits on the bed, then, without warning, falls back in a great heap. I gasp — then laugh. That is so…unexpected.

"They used to live on one of the neighboring islands," Stonehart explains. "They were terrified when they found out that somebody — a foreigner — bought their land. When I came here, and decided not to develop, they were beyond thrilled. Manuela begged me to let her work for me. She wouldn't take any money. She just wanted to show how much she appreciated the change of heart."

He rolls over and pops his head up to look at me. He seems almost a boy, carefree and unhurried. "Of course, I arranged things with Jose to make sure the family gets paid. We set up a trust for the kids. That's where the money goes. They don't need it for anything here. The islanders know how to get by. They fish and hunt for food, and have their own place a few miles inland. Jose has a kayak that connects him to the main island. Any time they need supplies — medicine, toiletries — that's where they go.

"It's a simple life. They thrive on it. If I had gone through with development, they would have lost it all. So yes, in that sense, Lilly…" a mischievous grin plays on his lips, "…they do see me as a hero. But — "

His gaze pierces me, sending a flush of arousal through my body.

" —I like it so much better when the words come from your lips."

***

"You can go anywhere your heart desires," Stonehart tells me some hours later, twining a finger through my hair.

In spite of the AC, we've both worked up quite a sweat. I feel a little tired, but content. Happy. Languid.

"Huh?" I say, barely following along. "What do you mean?"

"On the island, Lilly," Stonehart says. "Your collar

is deactivated. You don't have to wear the brooch. You can go explore as much as you want…" He trails a slow series of kisses down the side of my neck, over my shoulder, and down my arm. "So long as you don't try to escape."

An alarm goes off in my head. In an instant, all the comfort that I've been feeling is gone.

"Why would I try to escape?" I ask, trying to brush the suggestion off.

Stonehart gives a lazy smile. "Why, indeed. I trust that you won't. Besides, we're surrounded by the ocean. You wouldn't get far."

"Jeremy." I push myself up and look him deep in the eyes. "I am *not* going to make a runaway attempt."

A brief flash of surprise shows behind those pupils. It's quickly covered up.

"Good," he says. He sits up, swings his legs out of bed, stretches widely, and stands. On their own accord, my eyes travel to his firm butt. As Stonehart walks across the room to the bamboo cabinet, the muscles of his legs and back work in their full glory. He slips on a thin, blue robe.

A bit of disappointment bubbles up inside me. He really does have a fantastic body.

He turns to face me again while he works on the sash. "There are some things you want to watch out for," he warns. "Most of the wildlife is harmless. But there are some species of frogs that are poisonous. If you see any with yellow stripes on their backs, stay away. They won't attack, but if spooked, they might act in self-defense."

"I think I can handle a few wayward toads," I say. "I've dealt with more impressive predators in the past." I pause, trying to decide whether to voice the rest of my thoughts, and then just go for it. "Like you, for one."

"Like me?" Stonehart asks. "Why, Lily, that might just be the most flattering thing you've ever called me. It beats all those descriptions you dreamt up in the limo."

I cringe. "Please, can we not talk about that?" I ask. I get up, strut to him, and run a finger down his exposed chest. "I like it so much better when we're both here… in the moment… together…"

My hand keeps moving down his body. It glides over the tight grooves of his abs, then continues lower, and lower, and lower.

I bite my lip as I begin to stroke him. His sex starts to swell immediately in my palm.

"And I thought you'd had enough," he murmurs

in a low, raspy voice.

I shake my head. A diabolical excitement grows within me. "Nope."

"Woman, you keep acting like this—" I yelp as Stonehart sweeps me off my feet and carries me to the bed, "and I might never want to leave this island.

*So much the better,* I think slyly.

And I grab his hair and kiss him.

# Chapter Fifteen

The next few days pass like a dream. Stonehart wasn't kidding when he said his time here would be dedicated fully to me.

We go swimming. We sunbathe. We explore the wilderness in the back. I haven't encountered any yellow-stripped frogs—either figuratively or literally.

Stonehart is… well, the best way I can describe it is that he is finally *Jeremy*. Not Stonehart, but Jeremy. Not cold and calculating but deep, thoughtful, and kind.

If only things were always this way.

The children leave us alone the first day, probably on request of their parents. But, they reappear on the second, and every day thereafter.

Before setting foot on this island, I'd have expected Stonehart to be against such intrusions on our time together. But Jeremy, the new man I see who's evidence of yet another layer to his psyche, takes it all in stride. More than that. He loves it. He runs around on the beach with the boys, sits down and chats with the girl, helps her set out food, or drinks, or whatever other small errand her mother has delegated to her.

I learn their names. The boys are Aldo, Diego, and Matias. The girl is Luciana. I even pick up a few words of Hispanic: concha da mar, which means seashell, like the one I keep treasured as a gift, and muchacha bonita, which means something along the lines of "the most beautiful woman to walk the face of the earth."

Jeremy taught me that one.

Two days in, I go on an adventure in the wilds with two of the boys. They have a great time laughing at me when an enormous, red *something* bursts up from the ground and makes me shriek and drop down. Diego grabs my hand and points up, showing me the magnificent red parrot that's taken residence on one of the higher branches.

The kids, even though they're close to each other in age, are as different as can be. Matias, the youngest, is by far the biggest troublemaker. Diego, the one in the middle, is reserved and thoughtful... until something new and shiny grabs his attention, and then he's as spontaneous as can be. Aldo, who gave me the shell, is actually the quietest of the bunch. I can see how he takes care of his brothers and sister, as the oldest.

They're all best friends. I guess they have to be, with no other kids anywhere, but their affection for each other is contagious. I could tell, even if I never met Manuela or Jose, that they have great parents.

Taking a few hours each day to horse around with the kids is fun. It's also something I never, ever expected a chance to do—not while serving Stonehart's five years. But on this island, I'm learning how different things could be.

*Could.* That's the most important, operative distinction. Time here shows me how things *could be*, in a different life, in a different world, in a different existence.

It is not how things *are*. It's not going to fool me into wavering and forgetting my purpose when we return to America. That will never happen again.

That doesn't mean I can't enjoy myself for now. And I do. Immensely. Whether it's with Jeremy or with the kids, everything that happens feels like it's bathed in a soft, ethereal glow.

And speaking of Jeremy... well, like I said before, if we were in any other circumstance, the things he's been doing would be enough to make me start falling in love. He's sweet and compassionate. He places my needs and desires above his own.

Actually, that's not exactly true. Probably it's more that, so often, *his* desires line up quite well with mine.

He and I discover a hidden waterfall together, nestled deep in a lush, green forest glade. We climb to the top and look out, and then he surprises me — and makes my heart leap to my throat — when, laughing, he rips his shirt off and dives into the sparkling water below.

I rush to the edge and look down. All I can see is a small disturbance in the water where he dove in, quickly being obscured by the rushing stream from the waterfall.

"Are you insane?" I scream at him when he surfaces. "You could have gotten yourself killed! How'd you know the water wasn't shallow?"

He laughs and sweeps his wet hair back. "Don't act like that'd be such a great loss for you."

"It would!" I yell, trying hard to make my voice carry over the sound of the falling water. "If you die, I'd be stranded here!"

"Manuela and Jose would take care of you," he smirks. "Not that bad."

"Yeah, well, I don't want to be stranded on a remote Caribbean island forever!"

"You know what I think?" Jeremy asks.

"What?" I shoot back.

"I think that your concern for my well-being might actually be genuine."

"No shit it's genuine!" I yell, immensely annoyed with his casual nonchalance. I creep closer to the edge. "It—"

I don't get to finish my sentence. My foot slips on a wet rock and slides out from under me.

I fall hard on my butt. The air leaves my lungs in a grunt. Overpowering terror fills me as I start to slide forward on the down-slope. Before I can so much as scream, I'm hurtling off the ledge, falling through the air, reaching, grabbing, grasping for anything to stop my fall.

There's nothing. Cold air rushes over my face. The drop feels endless. My side collides with the hard surface of the water, at an impossibly awkward angle. Pain shoots through me, followed by an immediate numbness that encompasses the left half of my body. On instinct, I try to draw breath, but find nothing but water filling my mouth and nostrils .

I kick with all the strength in my legs, desperate for the surface. I spin too far and lose my orientation. I cannot tell up from down.

Panic overtakes me. I fight the water, clawing and kicking and twisting. But, the suffocating liquid surrounds me. My lungs cry out for air. The convulsive reflex makes me cough. More water rushes in.

I know, in the most pivotal place of my heart, that I am drowning.

Two strong hands grip me under the arms. A moment later — though it seems like a lifetime to my terror-stricken psyche — I break the surface.

I don't know what happens next. I have only a

moment before my oxygen-starved brain blacks out.

# Chapter Sixteen

I open my eyes slowly. It's dark. There's a harsh stinging in the back of my throat.

I hear the rustle of running feet, then a door open and closes. A moment later, a dim overhead light comes on.

"Lilly." It's Stonehart. His voice comes from behind me. I crane my neck to look back, but he's at my side in an instant.

He takes my hand and grips it tight. I can feel the stress pulsing through him. I look at him, then past him. It takes me a long time to recognize the space we're in as the bedroom.

"How did I get here?" I ask weakly.

"I carried you," he says. "I was so worried."

"About little old me?" I give a strained smile. I feel weak, probably from a mixture of dehydration, lack of food, and my most recent misadventure. "Hey, I'm tougher than you think."

"You've been out for two days," he tells me.

That's when I see his red-rimmed eyes. His untrimmed facial hair. His crumpled shirt.

He looks awful. Worse than I've ever seen him. Here is a man who looks like he has been to the precipice of hell and back.

"Lilly… what happened…. was my fault." His hand tightens around mine. "I was careless, and you got hurt. I can't forgive myself for that."

Of all the things he can be repentant about, he chooses *this*?

"I haven't left your side once," he tells me.

"Manuela and the others are in the adjacent room. They've been worried sick."

"Tell them… that I'm fine." I start to push myself up. "Just a little hungry."

"No." Stonehart's hands grip my shoulders. He eases me down. "Stay there. Don't move. Whatever you need, I'll get for you."

He's caring for me. *Again*. Somewhere deep inside, a tiny grain of hope emerges and tells me that maybe, this side of Stonehart is candid. Or at least, that it comes from an honest place of concern.

I settle back. There's a certain comfort knowing I'm being looked after by such a capable man. By Jeremy. Not by Rose, not by Stonehart, but by *Jeremy*.

I also find his concern to be very sweet. Nobody could fake such dedication. If he truly hasn't left my side once…

"Where were you when I woke up?" I ask suddenly.

"On the phone. Outside. I was about to order a chopper flown in to take you to a hospital. It's lucky you woke up when you did.

"Manuela checked on you when I brought you here. The islanders have more experience with water than anybody I know. They have to. Their lives revolve around it. When I told her what had happened, she examined you, and assured me you'd be fine. Eventually. But God knows what happened to you underwater. I couldn't tell if you hit your head or had a concussion. There wasn't any visible sign of damage, but still…"

He trails off, his jaw muscles working as he looks away. He seems to be on the verge of admitting something, maybe doing something, but is struck by indecision.

"Still what?" I ask quietly.

"Still, I didn't want to take the risk," he finally admits. By his expression and tone, I know that's not what he wanted to say originally. "I didn't know how you'd react if you woke up and found yourself in a hospital room. That was the last thing I wanted to subject you to."

*Because a hospital bed puts me outside of your control*, I think.

I keep my mouth shut.

"Manuela insisted that you'd be fine. But, every hour that passed put me more and more on edge. I set a deadline. If you didn't improve by nine tonight, I'd call the helicopter in."

"What time is it now?"

Stonehart leans forward and kisses my forehead. "Eight-twenty. You really know how to keep a man on edge."

"Huh." I look at the ceiling and consider everything he's said. Another half-hour, and I'd have been airlifted to Florida.

Is it a good thing that I woke up when I did? I don't know. Truth be told, coming to in a hospital room probably *would* have been traumatic. I'd have no idea how to act. What would I do, in my current state of mind, if I found myself surrounded by doctors and nurses and other people? What would they think about the collar? What would I be *allowed* to say? Would the brooch be on?

Maybe it's for the best that I woke up now. This way, there's no uncertainty. This way, I can stick to my original plan, without being tempted by new possibilities.

"There's something I've been waiting to do," Stonehart says, breaking into my thoughts. "I made the decision as I was carrying you back."

"Oh?" I look up at him, and see his unquestionable sincerity. My heart begins to flutter, just a little bit. "What?"

"One second." Stonehart glances over his shoulder. "I think you've got guests."

I lift my head and see Luciana peeking in from the door.

"Esta buena," Stonehart says. "Tell your family she wants to see them."

Luciana nods and runs off. Moments later, I'm surrounded by the family, relief mingling with concern on their features.

Manuela gives me something cold to drink, and helps bring the cup to my lips. Then she scolds her children for being too loud. I don't understand the words, but I can tell by their reaction.

I ask Stonehart to let her know that they're not a problem. He does, but still, after only a few minutes, Manuela takes everyone away and leaves me alone with Stonehart once again.

"I think you're their new favorite," he mutters as the door closes. "You've surpassed even me."

"I doubt anybody can ever do that," I say. "They owe their lives to you."

*Kind of like I do.*

"Hmm." He gazes at the door. After a minute, he walks over and locks it. "I don't want any interruptions," he says.

He turns to face me. There's a serious, almost solemn expression on his face. I've never seen Stonehart stressed — until now.

He looks visibly tired. That is by far a first.

It makes me realize that, somewhere deep down, he really is just a man. Sure, he can act the monster. He can be completely heartless and cold and without compassion… but all those faults come from somewhere. From some base that drives him to do what he does.

Stonehart is complicated. Nobody would ever deny that. Hell, even people who've only known him from afar would agree. But, I've seen all the different sides of him. I've seen him cold. I've seen him angry. I've seen him domineering, volatile, and unpredictable.

I've also seen him sweet. I've seen the kindness he

is sometimes capable of. It's not enough to overcome all the things he's done that exist at the other end of the spectrum. However, it's somehow reassuring to know that Yes, the capacity for kindness is still there. It hasn't been wiped away by the persona he's built for himself.

"Lilly." He says my name tenderly. Like a true lover. His voice, which has always held such power over me, affects me in the most primitive way.

I can't help but respond to it. It reaches into my soul and tugs on my very heartstrings — especially when my name comes from his lips, sounding like that.

"Yes?' I whisper. My heart is fluttering unsteadily in my chest. It adds to the anticipation of what it so come. I have no idea what that might be, but some intuition borne of being so long around Stonehart tells me it's not going to be bad.

"When you were out," he begins, walking slowly toward me, "I couldn't sleep. I didn't eat. My thoughts revolved solely around you. And all I felt was this overwhelming guilt. *I did this*, I told myself. *I am the one at fault.*"

I shake my head. "It's not like that. I don't blame you! It was an accident. I slipped and fell. Besides..." I swallow, remembering his arms catching me underwater, "...you saved me."

"You wouldn't have been in a position to need saving if it hadn't been for me!"

The outburst makes me shy back. He looks pained now, and angry. I can tell, however, that—for the first time—he's not angry with me, but with himself.

He takes a deep breath that makes his chest swell. "I'm sorry," he says. "You know how I hate to yell.

But Lily, around you… I feel emotions coming to life inside me that I haven't felt in years. In *decades*."

He sits on the side of the bed. He runs one hand through his hair, and looks into the distance when he speaks. The low light adds gravity to his words.

"You have to understand… who I am," he says. "And I cannot tell you everything. Not now. Not yet.

"But once I told you a story of my past. Of my father, of my brothers. I have not spoken to them since I was a teenager, you know.

"My whole life has been built around vengeance. I know it's a horrible thing to say, but I'm not one to mince words. Honesty, especially with yourself, is critical for a man of my position.

"I never thought I'd be admitting these things to another soul. I'm…" his long fingers tighten on the edge of the mattress, and he swallows, then he turns even farther away from me. "I'm not ready yet, Lilly. All I ask of you is a little patience. With me. Please."

He sounds so very sincere. No man can act this well. I decide that, holy shit, he *is* sincere.

I reach out and place one hand on top of his. He moves his head slowly, as if it's a great weight, and follows, from the shoulder down, the length of his arm. His eyes settle on our linked fingers. Then, after a somber moment, he raises his gaze to mine.

When I see his dark pupils, reflected in the flickering light, disbelief fills me. It might just be a trick of the dark, but I think that, for a moment, his eyes are actually glistening. Wet. As in, with tears.

He looks away before I can get a better read on it. But that brief glance is enough to make me feel like I've been run over by a truck.

*Stonehart, crying? Stonehart, showing one of the most*

*genuine of human reactions?*

I can't believe it.

He flips his hand over and takes hold of mine. Warmth creeps up my arm.

"I can do that," I say softly.

"Thank you," he says. Then he continues. "I wanted revenge against my father. I got that. I wanted revenge against my brothers. I got that, too. My life has been predicated on seeing justice done to those who've wronged me. It is what made me who I am. I offer no apologies for my actions. I live without regret. The only way to do that, however, is to bar yourself from the world. To live without emotion, without compassion. Without... love."

Abruptly, he stands. He begins to pace the room, his jaw clenching and unclenching between his stunted sentences.

"I did it all, you know. Everything I've ever wanted. I got for myself. The chips began to fall into place with the founding of Stonehart Industries. The name—that name—" he laughs without humor, " — was a childhood dream. I hated my real last name. *Hated* it. You know why, Lilly? Because I owed it to my father. Because it was a constant reminder of my link to him.

"Well, as soon as I could, I severed that link. I cut all ties to my family. To everyone… except the one person who treated me right. Except my mother."

"Do you still speak with her?" I ask.

"She's dead."

A deep silence fills the room. I feel ill. Queasy. What was I thinking, asking such a stupid question?

Stonehart walks to the cabinet and leans over it, supporting himself with his arms. He looks over his shoulder at me. The tears — the imagined tears? — are gone.

"Yes, Lilly, she's dead, and I was unable to prevent it. I could have helped her. If only I hadn't been so goddamned weak. So goddamned stupid. I could have saved her!"

"When?" I ask gently.

He snorts a sour chuckle. "More than twenty years ago. Not long after you were born. If I'd had five more years… hell, if I'd had *three*… I could have changed things. Maybe she would still be around today. But I did not have the power, twenty years ago, that I command today.

"I'm not talking about doctors or medical bills, Lilly. You know my father was rich. He had the means. My mother's death did not come from a want of resources. It came from something else.

Something… more ominous. A type of madness —
though none but I see it that way.

"Anyway." He shoves off and shakes his head.
"That's not what I meant to tell you. This isn't
supposed to be about me. It's supposed to be about
you. But…" He exhales, "…for you to understand, it
*has* to be about me. Don't you see? You, and your
effect on me."

Stonehart takes another deep breath. "Maybe it's
not about me any longer. Maybe it's about *us*. I've
never thought, before, of existing as a cohesive unit,
as being reliant on another person. I've never
thought of a relationship as worth more than just sex.
And you know," he smiles, "that I have an insatiable
appetite for that."

Heat floods my cheeks. He's certainly right in that
regard.

"My mother's death propelled me ever farther into the depravity I was building for myself. I had nothing left, so I attacked the world with a single-minded ferocity. I built my empire because it was all I could do.

"But it was more than that, Lilly. I found that I thrived on the competition. I thrived living on the edge. Building Stonehart Industries from the ground consumed me. It gave me purpose. It gave me goals. Clear, definable goals, where success could be measured in dollars and cents."

He chuckles. "Well. Maybe not cents. It's been a long time since I worried about cents."

"Material possessions were all I craved. I got all those. When I was younger, I thought they'd be enough to satisfy me. You've seen but a glimpse of the splendor I'm talking about. Cars, yachts, jets.

Estates in the country, in the mountains, apartments all over the word. New York, Paris, Sydney, Crete. Clothing. Beautiful women—most paid, some not. The reason for that," he clarifies, "is so that there could never be emotional attachment. Not from my end. I was never at risk for it. But *theirs*. Professional... models from Sweden, from Russia, from the East... also view sex as a business transaction.

"That's all I wanted. No complications. No feelings. No histrionics."

He sits down on the side of the bed. "I've had stalkers, Lilly. More than a handful. That is why I live the way I do. That is why my California estate is so secluded. What young, beautiful, but down-on-her-luck woman wouldn't want to be with me? What lengths would she not go through to nab the CEO of Stonehart Industries?

"I know who I am. I know my success makes me a magnet for the worst type of women. In my thirties… I made the mistake of letting one in. She almost ruined me."

"What happened?" I ask softly.

"Nothing relevant for you, my Lilly-flower," he says gently. Sweetly. "Especially because I vowed never to make a mistake like that again. I vowed, and I stuck to it. But this…" he turns over, and lowers himself beside me, "…us…*you*… This is no mistake."

His fingers brush my arm. I shiver.

"Stand up," he whispers.

I blink. He's just come closer, and now he wants me to stand?

But, something inside me propels me to do as he says without protest. I don't want to break the spell that's come over him.

"Stand before me." He sits up and places his feet on the ground. He tugs me between his legs, and caresses the side of my hips with both hands.

"You are lovely beyond compare," he says. "And when I thought I had lost you… when I thought that I might not see you awake again, I promised myself that I would mar your beauty, your innocence, your sweetness no longer. Do you know what I'm talking about, Lilly?"

"No." My voice sounds distant and soft, as if it's not even my own.

He takes my hands and brings them to his lips. He inhales deeply, then slowly starts to rise.

At full height, he towers over me. "I'm talking about…" his hands come up behind my neck. He touches the collar. "This."

My breath catches.

*He can't… he can't be doing… what I think he's doing.*

*Can he?*

"Tilt your chin up," he whispers.

I do. He does something with his fingers. A faint click sounds.

And the collar falls off.

Stonehart turns and places it on the bed. My hands shake badly as I bring them up to feel my neck. My fingers explore the spot where they expect to find that thin piece of plastic.

All they discover is my own smooth skin.

A choked sob rises out of me. Just one. My entire body feels light. Too light. As if it's not my own any longer. As if I'm… as if I'm…

As if I'm finally free.

Tears fill my eyes. My knees buckle.

Stonehart catches me before I can fall. He picks me up and handles me with the care given to a newborn child.

He walks with me slung across his arms and sets me on top of the desk. He touches the trail of wetness on my cheek. His thumb continues down my body. He slips off one strap of my top.

Lightly, his hands brush over my breasts.

"You," he says, "are so wonderful. And I promise you Lilly, that I will never mistreat you again."

And then we kiss, and I lose myself completely in his arms.

# Chapter Seventeen

Stonehart extends our stay on the island to make up for time lost.

No. Not Stonehart. Not any longer.

He's Jeremy now, both in my thoughts and in my speech. He's Jeremy, and I feel no qualms calling him that.

Everything feels wonderful. This really is a paradise, now. I'm free in mind, spirit, and body.

I soak up the sun and eat every bite of the exotic dishes Manuela prepares. At night, Jeremy and I make love. We drink. Either rum or tequila or wine or whatever other liquor he has in the house. We talk frivolities. We laugh.

With the collar gone, it's almost like a weight has

been lifted off Jeremy's shoulders. He is freer in his expressions with me than ever before. I don't get the sense that he's holding anything back. He's just being himself.

And that is a wondrous, wondrous thing.

There aren't any more confessions or revelations of the sort he gave the night he took the collar off. But I don't mind. There's an unspoken innocence to our interactions now.

One night, lying on the beach beside a great bonfire, Jeremy makes an unexpected announcement.

"Tomorrow evening," he says. "A helicopter will arrive and pick us up to bring us to the main island. There's a charity function that I've been asked to attend. They want me to speak. At first I said no, because I did not want to cut into my time with you, but I think, with all that's happened recently, we can risk a real public outing."

My eyebrows go up. " 'Risk' ?"

He motions lazily with his hand. "You know what I mean. In isolation, like this, we're fine. But we haven't yet attended a proper social function. There will be media there, Lilly. They will want pictures. It's all very glamorous, and I think it's about time that I am seen with you.

"Now." He turns to face me. "The question is: Are you ready to take the next step?"

"Yes," I answer resolutely.

"And…" his fingers touch my collarbone, "…are you able to guarantee your behavior? Or will you need," he frowns, and touches the spot just above the base of my throat, "the proper motivation?"

I sit up and look him square in the eyes. "Jeremy,"

I say. "I promise you, I will not do anything to compromise your position." I sweep my hair over one shoulder and adopt a haughty air. "I will be the most perfect companion for you tomorrow night."

"I hope so," Jeremy murmurs. "I really, really do."

***

The next day we're airlifted from our paradise and brought back to civilization.

Never in my wildest dreams did I think this would happen so soon. I'm going to a public gathering, with Jeremy, *without* the collar.

How much has the world changed since I've last been a part of it? How much of it has remained the same? The months I've spent in isolation can either be considered an eternity or a mere blip on the radar.

My nerves have been acting up all day. Jeremy says he trusts me. He acts like he trusts me. But there are layers and layers and layers to the man.

I haven't forgotten my resolve, my purpose, or my ultimate goal. Those things are always lurking in the back of my mind. Because of them, I have not once been able to achieve the type of carefree enjoyment on the island that Jeremy has.

They are the reason tonight has to be perfect. I cannot do anything that would betray Jeremy's trust, or make him suspect my true intentions. Because I know, it will take much longer than a week together for me to position myself in a spot where I can destroy him.

We land. The waiting limo takes us through busy streets. I miss all of it.

"Lilly." Jeremy touches my knee. "Relax. You look exquisite. You'll do fine. Remember the things we talked about, and there won't be any problems."

I squirm a little in my seat, and tug at the hem of my red silk dress. It doesn't even cover half my thighs.

*'The things we talked about.'* Jeremy's rules, which he articulated this morning.

Of course, I knew they were coming. Hearing them spoken aloud, however, reminded me exactly of the position I'm in.

They were simple, really, and not much of a departure from the ones he had established prior to our dinner in Portland.

Smile, but do not speak. If addressed, defer to him. Single-word answers are permitted. In conversation (which I should make every effort to avoid), be noncommittal. Never speak of my past, of my relationship with Jeremy, or of how we met. Do not volunteer personal information other than my first name.

"You'll be the perfect mystery," he announced. "Draped in red and black, you will dazzle them with your beauty and silent charm." Then he came close, and whispered in my ear, "Do not make me regret the choices I've made with you, for things that are done…" and he touched my neck, "…may yet be undone."

That was the only allusion he made to the collar. Past that, he left me alone to prepare.

We pull up in front of a lavish hotel. Crowds of people line the entrance. I see flashing lights from the paparazzi. Cameras. Expensive cars and velvet barriers. Stylish men and glamorous women, adorned with jewels of the type I've never seen outside of magazine ads.

I feel suddenly inadequate. I do not belong here. What do I know of celebrity, of the lives of the rich and famous?

"Ready?" Jeremy asks. He takes my hand. "It's show time."

We step out of the limo into a flurry of flashing lights and a cacophony of noise. I'm immediately thrown off balance by the fervor of it all, the commotion.

I cling to Jeremy's hand as my single lifeline. He guides me through the throng.

I hear his name being called out, again and again and again. He ignores the shouts. I hear questions about me: Who I am? Where did I come from? Jeremy pays them no mind as he leads me inside.

But mere feet from the door, a young reporter jumps the separating barrier and lands before us. He jabs a microphone into Jeremy's face like a weapon.

"Jeremy Stonehart," he demands. "Your company has faced immense public scrutiny after announcing intentions of an IPO last week. With the date for the public offering less than two months away, and all the recent controversy surrounding your operations in the Middle East, would you agree that it was a mistake to act so early?"

"No," Jeremy growls. He tries to step around the reporter, but he just parries with him.

"Stonehart Industries is a well-known public supporter of UNICEF. Don't you find such support highly disingenuous, in light of recent reports of your use of child slaves in Chinese mining operations?"

"That's false," Jeremy says. He looks around. "Can someone get this prick out of my face?"

"An explosion in a Pakistani textile factory recently claimed the lives of six hundred workers. The government claimed it was an accident, but my newspaper has uncovered massive oversights in factory safety conditions. My sources have discovered that this factory is owned by a subsidiary of Stonehart Industries. What compensation do you have planned for the families?"

"Those are baseless lies," Jeremy growls.

Blessedly, we escape inside. Jeremy is clearly agitated by the encounter. But, he covers it up the moment the doors close behind us.

The lobby is spectacular. All around me are beautiful, sophisticated people. There's a vibrant energy to the room that comes from the hum of conversation. It's a stark departure from the commotion outside, but no less exciting.

Jeremy leads me through, stopping to greet some people, being hailed and stopped by others. In here, he makes time for them all.

I play my role to perfection. I smile graciously and accept the compliments given me. But as we swim through the crowd, pausing here and there for a few words, I start to understand why Jeremy felt it was safe to bring me.

It's because I don't matter. Nobody in here cares who I am. The men all want to talk to Jeremy. The women couldn't give two shits about me — except to shoot some envious glares when they think I'm not looking.

Outside, it was different. The media throng was only there for frivolous details like who arrived with whom and to compete for the most scandalous photographs. Inside, the people are classy, and beyond such interests. To them, I am little more than a wall decoration. A pretty bird to sit on Jeremy's shoulder and repeat the obligatory thank you's following the throwaway remarks on my dress, my hair, my youth. They're all empty words, of course. These people know that I do not matter.

It's slightly galling to be the subject of such passive disrespect. But would I want things any different? No. This way, there can be no mistakes. This way, I can further Jeremy's trust in me, little by little.

Eventually, we end up in the dining room. There's a stage set in front with a podium for the speakers. For Jeremy.

The MC announces the start of dinner.

"We are honored to have a special guest tonight," he says into the microphone. "His appearance has already caused quite a stir. I'd like to invite all of you to join me in welcoming to the stage, President, CEO, and founder of Stonehart Industries, Mr. Jeremy Stonehart!"

Jeremy stands to a massive round of applause. He is a vision in his crisp, black suit, his perfect hair, his skin tanned from our time in the sun. He breathes in the attention given to him like a rock star.

*This is his environment*, I find myself thinking. *This is where he excels*.

He makes his way to the stage and shakes hands with the MC. He steps before the mic, and the applause continues.

He taps it twice. "Yes, yes," he acknowledges. "I know you love me. But please, save the applause for when I do something really special."

Laughter. He has made a joke. Jeremy Stonehart, starting his speech with a joke. I never thought I'd see the day.

From that point on, everything passes in a blur. Jeremy returns to me after he finishes his presentation. I gush at how powerful it was, how moving, at how the audience clung onto his every word.

He smirks, now full of hubris, and says, "Well, did you expect anything different?"

A live auction follows. It provides our entertainment during dinner. The grand item up for bid is a weekend retreat to the Alps, valued at just over $25,000. All proceeds to charity.

Jeremy bids half a million and wins.

It's only after dinner is over, and we are free to mingle, that disaster strikes.

Jeremy and I are exploring the crowd. He is being congratulated on his speech, on the news of Stonehart Industries going public, on his supreme generosity at the auction. I'm but a shadow on his arm, invisible to all…

Or so I think.

Out of nowhere, I hear my name being called out.

"Lilly! Oh my gosh, Lilly, is that really you?"

I freeze. Terror fills me. Stonehart is too engaged in his current conversation to have noticed. I start to turn, but before I get even halfway around a pair of long, elegant arms throw themselves around my neck.

I'm let go. A woman, maybe a decade older than

Jeremy, stands beaming before me.

Her dark skin contrasts with her white dress and makes her shine with radiant beauty. Her hair is different from the last time I saw her. It's now blonde.

That doesn't stop me from recognizing her right away.

It's Thalia. Fey's mom.

But what is she doing here —

Of course. Fey has rich parents. It makes sense that they'd have connections required to attend events like this one.

Yet what are the odds of her running into *me* here?

Jeremy, by now, is aware of the disturbance. He turns to Thalia. His eyes flash at me, demanding an explanation.

I want nothing more than to turn away and pretend I don't know her. But it's too late for that now.

"Lilly, it's so good to see you!" Thalia exclaims. "I can't believe I found you here. And you're with —"

She looks at Jeremy. Her eyes widen in perceptible shock.

"Jeremy Stonehart," he says smoothly, offering her his hand. As she shakes it, her eyes go back to me, full of disbelief.

"Jeremy Stonehart," she repeats under her breath. "I saw you on stage. You were spectacular. My husband speaks of your company all the time."

"Does he?" Jeremy murmurs. "Would I happen to know the man?"

"Oh no." Thalia shakes her head. "No, no. He's

just a simple—a banker."

"Lilly," Jeremy says to me. "I think it's customary for you to introduce me to your friend."

"Oh!" I come to myself with a little jump. I didn't even notice that Thalia had forgotten to give her name. Her shock at finding me with Jeremy Stonehart must really be something.

"This is Thalia Rosene. She's the mother of one of my old college roommates at Yale."

Mention of the university sparks Thalia.

"Fey told me you had disappeared. After you went to work in California, you never called, or emailed, or texted. We all assumed you just got so busy working, but clearly…" she sneaks a sidelong look at Jeremy, full of hidden meaning, "…you've managed to integrate yourself into the world you've always dreamed of very well."

332

I hate the accusation in her words. The silent insinuation. The suggestion that I forsook my closest friends just to be close to Stonehart. That I am nothing more than a gold digger.

"Lilly's done much more than that, Thalia," Stonehart says. "She's been an absolute star at Corfu Consulting. Already, her work is the stuff of legends."

I stiffen at the easy way the lies spill from his lips.

"Well, I certainly wouldn't expect anything less of our Lilly," Thalia says smartly. "We all know how driven she is."

She turns to me. "Fey is going to be so excited when I tell her that you're here."

My stomach, which I thought couldn't go any lower, sinks all the way to my toes. "Fey is... here?" I ask weakly. I feel sick.

"Not *here* at the gala, no. But she's on the island with us. She's staying at the resort. I just know she'd love to see you. You two have so much to catch up on! How about it. Tomorrow morning? Are you free for breakfast? Do you have a cell phone? Oh, what am I asking, of course you have a cell phone." She digs out her own from her purse. "Here, quick, give me your new number. Fey told me the old one doesn't ring anymore."

I look at Jeremy, desperate for an escape. He gives it without pause.

"Here," he says, handing Thalia a business card. I recognize it as the same one I was not supposed to be given in his San Jose office so very long ago. "That has my personal line on the back. Give me a call to arrange the meeting. I would be delighted to meet one of Lilly's old friends."

Thalia gives me a curious look, but takes the card and deposits it into her wallet.

"I'll call tomorrow morning," she says.

Stonehart gives a broad smile. Looking at him, you would never expect anything is wrong. "Lilly and I will be looking forward to it. It was a pleasure to meet you, Thalia."

And with that one sentence, he's dismissed her. He doesn't turn away, or direct his attention elsewhere, but the meaning behind his words is clear.

"The pleasure's all mine," Thalia murmurs. She shoots me another curious look, and then glances over her shoulder. "I think I hear my husband calling. Excuse me."

And she turns around and hurries into the crowd.

I watch her go in a stunned silence.

*What now?*

Jeremy's hand tightens on my arm. It's enough to bruise.

"We're leaving," he hisses in my ear. "Now."

He pulls me after him, ignoring calls to stop and chat. Once we're out in the cool night air, he takes out his phone and dials the limo.

Our ride arrives minutes later. Despite the warm night air, goose bumps line my exposed skin,.

We get into the car. Jeremy remains silent. His jaw is tight, and his eyes are dark.

He terrifies me.

We stop in front of a grand, towering structure a few blocks away. It's another hotel. Jeremy still hasn't said a word. I have no idea what's going through his mind.

I can't take the uncertainty anymore. "Jeremy, I swear," I plead, "I didn't—"

"*Enough.*" He cuts me off with a savage scowl. "The hand has been dealt. The stage is set. Appearances must be maintained. Tomorrow…" his eyes bore into me, "Will be your greatest test. There will be rules. *Strict* rules, Lilly."

A shiver of fear runs down my spine as I get shades of the man I first met, bound to the pillar, so many months ago. Shades of Stonehart.

"We will meet your friend and her family. But Lilly." He pauses. The shadows emphasize the hard features of his face.

"If so much as one toe steps out of line… Well, nothing that you've been subject to in the past will compare to what I'll do to you then."

## The End.

# Mailing List Sign-up

Don't want to miss the release of the next book?
Sign up for my **email list** (http://eepurl.com/z-Lgv)
and be the first to know about my new books.

## *Uncovering You 6* **comes out summer 2014.**

# Enjoyed this book?

If you enjoyed this book, the best place to let me know is on my Facebook page:

www.facebook.com/ScarlettEdwardsAuthor

I post tons of teasers, book excerpts, pictures, and lots of other fun stuff. We're building an active community of *Uncovering You* addicts on there, so come join us! It's also the best place to correspond directly with me.

Hope to see you there,

Scarlett

Made in the USA
Lexington, KY
02 March 2015